100 Ideas for Teaching Physical Development

Also available from Continuum

100 Ideas for Teaching

Physical Development

Simon Brownhill

continuum

Continuum International Publishing Group

The Tower Building   80 Maiden Lane
11 York Road   Suite 704
London   New York
SE1 7NX   NY 10038

www.continuumbooks.com

British Library Cataloguing-in-Publication Data
A catalogue record for this book is available from the British Library.

ISBN: 9-781-8470-6193-5 (paperback)

Designed and typeset by Kenneth Burnley, Wirral, Cheshire
Printed and bound in Great Britain by MPG Books Ltd, Bodmin, Cornwall

Contents

Section 4: Using Equipment and Materials

Section 5: Challenges for Physical Development

Section 6: Movements: Developmental Stages

Section 7: Learning and Teaching in Physical Development

Section 8: Links with Other Areas and Aspects of Learning and Development

Acknowledgements

There are many people who deserve my sincere thanks for their support, guidance and advice in the preparation, writing and editing of this book:

- Christina Garbutt at Continuum for asking me to write this book – thank you for your continued belief in me
- Jane Key at Hardwick Primary School for giving me some areas for consideration to get me started!
- Suzanne Meehan, Janet King and Tracey McDonnell at Derby City Council – thank you for your recommendations, suggestions and the time you gave up for me
- Gemma Brownhill and Phil 'the Simpson' Hewitt for your activity suggestions
- Marissa Webb, Alistair Crawford and Mark Woodfield for kindly supporting the editing process – thanks for making my drivel comprehensible
- My fabulous family – thank you for your continued love and support
- My second family – thank you for continuing to be a part of my life
- My wealth of fantastic friends – thank you for being great people
- All of the colleagues and students I know and work with at the University of Derby – it really is a privilege working for/with you
- The reader for putting your hand in your pocket and adding a few more pennies to my royalty cheque – I feel another pair of socks coming on!
- And finally, to the little boy I watched doing the Stomp dance in Nice airport – thanks for giving me the idea of bringing the West End stage into early years settings.

Thank you all very much indeed.

SPB

To Emily 'Bullock'

In loving memory of Mrs Griffiths and Deca

Introduction

So, what's the story?
Open any newspaper or magazine today and you are certain to find articles or reports on any of the following: childhood obesity; rising levels of heart disease, diabetes and other medical disorders in the youth of today; the poor eating and drinking habits of both children and adults; and declining percentages of people engaging in physical activity. It certainly does not make pleasant reading, especially when one considers the current and long-term implications of these trends: rising levels of behavioural difficulties in young people, poorer interpersonal skills between children and adults, adults leading a poorer quality of life as they battle with illness and health problems, and people having shorter life spans.

So, why is this happening?
Over the past 30 years there have been huge technological and cultural changes that have transformed the lifestyles of people all across the world. Many of us own televisions, mobile phones and computers, all of which we now could not live without. While these have been largely beneficial, many of us have failed to notice the way they have damaged the social, emotional and cognitive development of children. Nowadays, childhood can be characterized by sedentary activity filled with Xboxes and other computer gaming, DVDs, iPods, and the internet. The world has become fast paced and so has food; fast food restaurants such as McDonald's and Burger King are everywhere. Colourful fizzy drinks line shop shelves, hundreds of different bars of chocolate call out to us through powerful advertising campaigns to consume them, and crisps and other snacks are readily available for those who need to 'eat and run'. Finally, with more and more reports of children being either kidnapped or killed on the roads, parents and carers are understandably reluctant to allow their children to 'go out and play'.

So, what can be done about this?
For many children today, their only favourite physical activities are fingers, eyes and mouth exercises: computer gaming and eating snacks while watching television. This needs to change, and it needs to change now. We need to switch those electronic screens off and get children 'up and doing and moving', both inside and outside. We need to develop not only their health and well-being but also their emotional and social well-being through physical activity. We need to replace those pre-packaged foods we put in front of children and offer them fresh fruit, vegetables and unprocessed food full of vitamins, minerals and wholesome goodness. We need to encourage children to drink more water. We need to do it now.

So, what are the benefits of doing this?
To answer this I present a beautifully succinct series of adapted points presented by Kit (2008):

1. A child who engages in physical activity regularly is more likely to continue exercising even as an adult.
2. Physical activity helps children achieve and maintain a healthy body weight.
3. Regular physical activity helps build and maintain strong, healthy muscles, bones and joints.
4. Physical activity aids in the development of important interpersonal skills such as team building. This is especially true for participation in team sports.
5. Physical activity helps improve the quantity and quality of sleep.
6. Research has shown that physical activity promotes improved school attendance and also enhances academic performance.
7. Children who engage in regular physical activity tend to have greater self-esteem, greater confidence and a better self-image.
8. Participating in regular physical activity prevents or delays the development of many chronic diseases such as heart disease, diabetes, obesity and hypertension, and promotes health.
9. Children who are active report fewer symptoms of anxiety and depression and have better mental control.
10. Physical activity helps improve motor coordination and enhances the development of various motor performance skills.

So, where do I fit into all of this?
We need to change children's behaviours and do it when they are in their infancy. This is where you, the dedicated, hardworking and wonderful practitioners taking the time to read this introduction, fit in. You have possibly one of the most important roles to play in the fight to get the adults of the future fit, healthy and active. With your determination, expertise and drive you can get the children you have the privilege of working with puffing, panting and loving moving.

So, what's this book going to do for me?
This book is written specifically to support those practitioners who want the best for the children they support, irrespective of whether they work with one child at home or with 120 in a Foundation unit. It has not been written to be revolutionary or cutting edge, but it has been written with quality in mind. It explores both the simple yet successful practice that for many years has set the standard for practitioners and settings in the early years, and new, exciting and innovative ideas to breathe life into policy and practice across all aspects of learning and development for Physical Development in the Early Years Foundation Stage (EYFS) (DfES, 2007). It aims not only to provide you with activities and suggestions that you can immediately take to the 'shop floor', but also to share with you information, thoughts and considerations to develop your personal philosophy towards children's physical development while helping you to reflect on,

develop and enrich EYFS planning, provision, learning and teaching, and assessment. Please do not see this book as another 'tips for practitioners' epic. It has been deliberately written to make you 'stop, consider and implement' with the needs of your children in mind, and it is hoped that you, as a practitioner, will adopt this mindset when engaging with this text.

So, what is special about this book?
This book does contain 100 Ideas, but these are *broad* ideas that are intended to drive effective provision. Each main Idea is presented in the initial introductory paragraph. The bullet points below this are a collection of suggestions that will allow the main Idea to become a reality. Attempting to provide ideas specific to a particular setting with a particular age group is virtually impossible, thus the suggestions, which span the 0–5 age phase, can be dipped into, encouraging the reader to be selective in their choice as to how they would like to put the Idea into practice.

Please adapt, alter and amend suggestions so that they are fit for purpose. This approach is designed to build a level of critical thinking in those engaging with this text, promoting discussion, debate and analysis on a personal and professional level with others so that only the very best suggestions are used, so as to have the most impact on the physical development of those children engaging with them.

So, what should I remember about this book?
It is important to remember that this book is not 'the answer' to all the issues, concerns and debates surrounding physical development in young children today. Instead, it serves as a 'PE store of suggestions' so that practitioners, parents and carers, and other adults are aware of what should be going on in their settings and what can be done to ensure that the young children they work with have the best physically active time that is humanly possible.

So, go forth . . . and move!

List of Abbreviations

The following abbreviations are used throughout this book:

Key Stages and age phases
EYFS   Early Years Foundation Stage (0 to 5+ years)
KS1   Key Stage 1 (5 to 7 years)
KS2   Key Stage 2 (7 to 11 years)

Areas of learning and development
PSED   Personal, Social and Emotional Development
CLL   Communication, Language and Literacy
PSRN   Problem Solving, Reasoning and Numeracy
KUW   Knowledge and Understanding of the World
PD   Physical Development
CD   Creative Development

Settings
F1   Foundation 1 (formerly known as Nursery classes)
F2   Foundation 2 (formerly known as Reception classes)

ELG   Early Learning Goal

DfES   Department for Education and Skills
DCSF   Department for Children, Schools and Families

ECM   Every Child Matters

PHSCE   Personal, Health, Social and Citizenship Education

SEN   Special Educational Needs

Section 1:
Introducing
Physical Development

Why the Need for Physical Development?

Ask yourself the following: can you tie a shoelace? Can you walk across a room in a straight line? Can you go up and down stairs with ease? Clearly, as adults, we have built up sophisticated skills in movement, negotiation and manipulation to be able to undertake these activities with 'mastered precision'. Young children, however, simply do not have these capabilities. This is why it is so important for children to engage in purposeful, challenging and exciting physical activity.

● *Movement for the fun of it.* Set up activities that allow children to feel the freedom and enjoyment of moving. For example, they could build towers out of cardboard boxes to jump off; splash and kick water in the paddling pool; and use dance-like movements to greet each other rather than using spoken words.

● *Learn by being active.* Simply encouraging children to go and run outside supports them to practically appreciate the effects of exercise on their bodies and the Personal, Social and Emotional Development (PSED) benefits of running around with others, which in turn helps to build a sense of achievement and well-being.

● *Up! Do! Move!* Plan physically active adult-led activities as opposed to sitting down 'chalk and talk' delivery, which can result in young children sitting for unnecessary amounts of time. For example, teach simple counting through movement: *one* star jump, *two* claps, *three* nods of the head, *four* knee bends . . .

● *Move yourself.* Model movements so children have something to base their own movements on. An example would be babies learning to crawl.

IDEA 2

The Goodness of Physical Development in Young Children's Lives

As is highlighted in the Introduction to this book, Physical Development (PD) plays an essential part in helping to support the lives of children in terms of being physically active. The media coverage of overweight and obese children is constant, but there are many other reasons why the development of a healthy and active way of life is important, and these should drive the reasoning behind practice.

- *Obesity*. Statistics continually change regarding the percentages of children who are considered to be overweight or obese by the age of 7. All we need to remember is that the prevalence of obesity increases with age, therefore having a good run around or doing 15 star jumps every day is very important.

- *Bone density*. Research has shown that exercise is more effective than calcium in increasing bone density. Get your young children jumping, running, bounding and stamping to make those bones big and strong.

- *Preventing disease*. Obesity in adults can increase the likelihood of their developing diabetes, high blood pressure, heart disease and respiratory infections. Getting involved with the children as they engage with their PD will help your life as well.

- *Muscle strength*. Physical activity helps to strengthen and build children's muscles, enabling them to move more quickly and with greater confidence. While we do not want to turn our young children into bodybuilders, muscle tone is all for the good, so encourage them, where appropriate, to help you lift and carry resources for others to use.

- *Self-esteem*. Children with high self-esteem are able to achieve anything they want to, because they have the self-belief and determination to succeed. Physical activity plays a vital role in building this self-realization, so make them feel good about themselves by setting realistic personal challenges.

- *Gross and fine motor movements*. Babies and young children need lots of opportunities to practise, hone and develop limb–eye coordination, dexterity and large movements with their bodies. Provide such opportunities through a balance of indoor and outdoor provision.

IDEA 3

What Physical Development Means for Children in the Early Years

Children in the Early Years Foundation Stage (EYFS) are keen to engage in anything physically oriented, mainly because movement is as natural and essential to their lives as are love, care, rest and nutrition. For young children to get the best out of life, PD should drive the following:

- *Activity.* Encourage children to engage in large-movement household tasks such as cleaning, cooking, washing and drying in the setting so that a 'purpose' to movement and action is developed. Learning to make small movements with books – holding them correctly, turning the pages and interacting appropriately with the flaps and tabs – is a very important activity too.

- *Challenge.* Provide frequent opportunities for children to cut out shapes with various cutting implements, use knives and forks to eat with, skip (on their own and with ropes), and develop an effective grip in using writing and art tools, which most children notoriously find a challenge.

- *Confidence.* Build self-esteem levels by allowing babies and children to move and wriggle, run freely, climb with safety in mind, pour drinks for others, and steer tricycles around obstacle courses.

- *Imagination.* Encourage children to become characters (e.g. the pig from the story *The Pig in the Pond*) or objects (e.g. bubbles), and enter into situations (e.g. escaping from the Giant's lair), to build up exciting ways of moving.

- *Safety.* Actively support and remind children about appropriate ways of washing and drying their hands, putting their feet squarely on the pedals of trikes, and being aware of 'hot spots' where they are not allowed to play.

- *A positive sense of well-being.* Plan activities that help children to work as a team, cooperating, sharing and taking turns with others. Work to ensure there are lots of 'puff and pant' activities to bring some rosy colour to children's faces.

IDEA 4

The Four Themes of the EYFS and Physical Development

The four key themes which express the principles that underpin effective practice in the EYFS are designed to guide the work of all early years practitioners. It is therefore important to develop an idea of how these can drive (and potentially already are driving) standards for Learning, Development and Care across the EYFS age phase.

- *A unique child.* Plan activities that develop a sense of confidence and achievement from what the child can already do. For example, once young children are able to grasp and hold on to objects, encourage them to post the objects into containers. Build competencies by ensuring that activities are based on active participation. For example, share oral suggestions to help children to throw beanbags a greater distance, combining these with demonstrations and opportunities for children to put them into practice.

- *Positive relationships.* Work with parents and carers so that they appreciate the value and importance of PD in their child's life. Encourage them to be active with their babies and young children outside of the setting – see Ideas 94 and 96. Build strength and confidence by modelling actions and techniques, playing *with* and *alongside* children. Use verbal and non-verbal strategies to motivate and excite.

- *Enabling environments.* Work collaboratively with practitioners, parents and carers, other settings and external professionals to provide a stimulating environment for children to play in that is safe, secure and challenging – see Idea 91. Ensure that children have daily planned access to outdoor play areas irrespective of the weather (settings in Norway do it, so why can't we?).

- *Learning and development.* Use cross-curricular links to strengthen and validate learning experiences – see Section 8. Strive for different types of play to permeate through planning for PD, based on the needs of the children. Use open-ended questioning – Who . . . ? What . . . ? Where . . . ? Why . . . ? How . . . ? When . . . ? – to stimulate creative and critical thinking. Appreciate the importance of having a good understanding of child development, recognizing the value of differentiation (see Idea 87) and quality-first teaching to support practice.

IDEA 5

Physical Development and the Commitments for Themes 1 and 2 of the EYFS

'A Unique Child' and 'Positive Relationships' are invaluable themes that support children in their PD. The four commitments that drive each theme are able to work individually or in partnership with others to strengthen Learning and Development. But what do these commitments look like in practice, particularly in relation to Physical Development?

- *Child development.* Babies and children develop physically at different rates and in different ways. Differentiate in terms of resources, ability, age, expectations, support and levels of encouragement (see Idea 87).

- *Inclusive practice.* Embrace diversity by valuing and integrating community movement, for example bhangra dancing, into the curriculum (see Idea 30).

- *Keeping safe.* Protect children by using well-made resources, mats and aprons, and teach practices linked to lifting, lowering and using large and small pieces of equipment (see Idea 34).

- *Health and well-being.* Work with the children to keep the setting clean and safe, providing open access to the outdoor play area even if it is drizzling outside (see Idea 88).

- *Respecting each other.* Build honest and warm relationships with children so that you can give them practical help and emotional support with ease (see Idea 70).

- *Parents as partners.* Reflect on the quality and quantity of suggestions made linked to Ideas 96 and 97 in ensuring that you regard parents as partners.

- *Supporting learning.* Learn to step back and watch children, giving them time and space to develop physical skills, knowledge and understanding. Offer appropriate challenges and new learning where appropriate (see Idea 67).

- *Key person.* Support babies and children in being confident in engaging in PD activities through constant reassurance, encouragement and comfort (see Idea 47).

The Commitments for Themes 3 and 4 and Physical Development

'Enabling Environments' and 'Learning and Development' are the remaining two themes that drive EYFS policy and practice. Their associated commitments (see Idea 5) are invaluable in assuring quality provision and experiences for children linked to PD; let's examine these in turn.

- *Observation, assessment and planning.* Starting points for PD should always be from where the child is at; for example, if a child is interested in superhero play, use this as a way of developing gross motor skills, such as by exploring different ways of travelling to catch the baddy.

- *Supporting each child.* Practitioners should plan and provide for each child, depending on that child's 'learning journey'. Meet individual needs through personalized activities and one-to-one support.

- *The learning environment.* The emotional, indoor and outdoor environment has a real impact on children's physical development. Help children to feel safe and secure, yet brave and adventurous, when using large and small resources through your generous use of praise, encouragement and empathy.

- *The wider context.* Build effective communication links with parents, other settings, professionals, individuals and groups or establishments within the community, such as health visitors, doctors and sports centres, to form partnerships to tackle childhood obesity, and support progress towards the five outcomes of Every Child Matters (ECM) (DfES, 2004).

- *Play and exploration.* Various types of play, such as solitary, collaborative and rough-and-tumble, should be promoted through the physical development activities provided, both indoors and outdoors. Work to plan for these.

- *Active learning.* PD requires movement, be it large or small; active learning supports this. Enough said.

- *Creativity and critical thinking.* Set creative challenges, such as 'How many different ways can you go down the slide?' or 'How might you move through the obstacle course with one body part always on the floor?', while asking questions to promote thinking, such as 'Can you throw the beanbag further before or after snack time?' or 'Who can jump the highest? Why do you think that?'

- *Areas of learning and development.* See Section 8 for more details.

The Relationship between Physical Literacy and Physical Development

Physical literacy is focused on the development of fundamental movement and sports skills in children and young people – see www.physical-literacy.org.uk. Research has shown that many children will withdraw from physical activity, becoming more inactive and making unhealthy choices in their later life, if they fail to develop physical literacy. Therefore, integrating this into your policy and provision is considered to be best practice at this present time.

- *Ground, snow, ice and water.* Children need to develop their skills in these four environments. Consider which areas dominate your physical development provision at present. How could you introduce more opportunities for children to work in snow or on ice?

- *Run like the wind.* Encourage children to run not only in straight lines but with stops, starts and changes in direction. Tag and chasing games are great ways to achieve this.

- *Body shape play.* Engage children with activities that support them in making body shapes and movements. Have them pretend to slither like a snake and roll like a rolling pin on the floor or down a small grassy slope.

- *Quiet times.* For quiet times, or when in small spaces, play balancing games. For example, the children could stand on one foot with one hand on top of their heads. Try balancing on different body parts – hands, knees, bellies, backs, tiptoes – working to build confidence and capabilities.

- *Jumping games.* Have them jump up, making shapes in the air. See how high the children can jump, or how far. Have them try jumping from one foot or from both at the same time.

- *Cycling activities.* Riding a tricycle or a bike – with or without training wheels – will develop children's dynamic balance.

IDEA 8

The Link Between Physical Development and Standards

There is no secret: physical development can raise educational standards. As every setting and provider is to be inspected regarding the quality of its early years provision, it is no surprise that practitioners are striving to raise standards in all areas of Learning and Development. So what can physical development do and how?

- *Ready to learn?* A bit of Brain Gym® (visit http://esl.about.com/od/ englishlessonplans/a/braingym.htm) and Wake and Shake (www.youthsporttrust.org) can get children in the mood for learning. Try it throughout the day and watch the children reap the benefits of their engaged attitudes. Activ8 (www.activ8.org) is an exciting alternative.

- *Will your handwriting be legible?* Encourage the rotation of the shoulders and arms (play Windmills, in which children's arms whirl backwards, forwards and in opposite directions, both individually and at the same time) and wrists and fingers (try threading, cutting with scissors, and painting) so that children will build up increasing control and confidence using writing implements.

- *'What wonderful vocabulary you have, my dear.'* Physical activity encourages children to listen to, use and interpret language. Engage children in dance (Whirl! Flutter! Shrivel! Bound!), challenges ('How could you get down the ladder using only one arm?') and game play ('Can you explain to me the rules of Squigglehop?') for purposeful language use.

- *Being brilliantly behaved.* One of the hardest things for young children to do is sit still, so build this up gradually, encouraging them to be well behaved for 3 minutes on the carpet, then 4, then 5 . . .

- *Reading for a purpose.* Encourage children to read signs, labels on boxes and gaming instructions to raise standards and expectations linked to reading.

Movement Milestones

Practitioners and parents and carers are likely to be aware of movement 'milestones': broad age-related expectations for the developing child that all children are checked against. Awareness of the progressive sequence of development and activities associated with these milestones is very important not only for practitioners but also for parents and carers:

- *Birth to the first few weeks.* Have soft toys and rattles to hand to encourage development of the baby's reflex actions.

- *3 to 6 months.* Use sounds, voices and toys to promote the lifting of the head while supporting the baby to sit on their own or against an object.

- *6 to 8 months.* Support the baby in sitting up unaided. Demonstrate how to pass objects between hands, giving them encouragement.

- *8 to 12 months.* Provide plenty of space for children to crawl. Play 'creepy crawlies' by allowing the child to creep away from you while you creep slowly after them. Support them in walking but take care of the environment as they begin to pull themselves up to a standing position. Cloths on dining room tables are certain to be pulled off!

- *12 to 18 months.* Man those stairs or steps, thus allowing the child to climb them unaided and creep backwards down them. Encourage them to walk unaided between objects, people and spaces.

- *24 to 36 months.* Ask children to help you at snack time, opening bottles of milk, cutting bread into squares or triangles and washing up crockery to develop those fine motor skills.

- *36 to 48 months.* Play 'Peek-a-boo', encouraging children to creep up on you from afar, tiptoeing, running, stopping and coming downstairs in a quest to get you!

- *40 to 60 months.* Get up and go! Let those feet move in different ways, at different speeds, along with hopping, jumping and tricycle riding.

Adapted from Woodfield, L. (2004) *Physical Development in the Early Years.* London: Continuum.

Activities and Games from the PE Store 1

In order for practitioners to effectively ensure quality provision in their settings, there is a real need for innovative and exciting activities to engage children in purposeful physical activity. This is where this Idea fits in; it simply acts as a collection of wonderful, wacky and weird activities that are sure to get children active.

- *Strictly Movement.* Bring *Strictly Come Dancing* and *Dancing on Ice* into the setting by providing space for children to move to music in the style of a rumba, a cha-cha or freestyle.

- *Fine motor manipulation.* Help children to develop their fine motor skills by inviting them to create pegboard patterns, complete jigsaws or fasten elastic bands to safe pegboards.

- *Funky bedding.* Create paper bedding for the setting's hamster by cutting along different lines (zigzag, wiggly, ripply, straight and curved) to create different-shaped offcuts.

- *Chase games.* Teach children how to play Cops and Robbers, Stig in the Dump and other games that encourage chasing, dodging and catching skills.

- *Just keep rolling.* Support children in using their bodies to represent objects that roll, such as a snowball going down a hill, a car without its handbrake on or a ball of dung being pushed by a beetle.

- *West End calling.* Play music from different musicals that have big dance numbers for the children to enjoy and move to, such as *Beauty and the Beast*, *Stomp* and *Hairspray*.

Section 2:
Exploring Movement
and Space

IDEA

11

Types of Movement

While practitioners appreciate that there are many different ways in which young children should be able to move, there are few who are aware of the three main types of movement that children need to gain experience of: posture (stability), travelling movements (locomotion) and contact with objects (manipulation). Ensure that these types of movement actually take place in our settings by using any of the following suggestions:

- *Don't forget to warm up.* Provide opportunities for children to stretch, twist and turn prior to physical activity, focusing on different parts of the body. Build up a warm-up routine, adding music where appropriate.

- *'Reach that for me, would you?'* Set up challenges whereby children have to collect items from lying, sitting and standing positions.

- *Cat and Mouse.* Divide the children into two groups with one group having tags hanging out of the back of their shorts (the tails of the 'mice'). The other group (cats) have to grab the tags by alternately running, hopping and galloping after the mice as quickly as they can.

- *Monkey Business.* Have the children use monkey bars, ladders and climbing frames to imitate the movements and behaviours of gorillas and chimpanzees.

- *Spider-person.* Put jumping movements into a lively context through role play. The children can jump up on to imaginary walls and across the tops of buildings like Spiderman.

- *Puppy play.* Encourage children to pretend they are puppies or the puppy's owner, throwing, catching, rolling and stopping imaginary or real Frisbees, balls and toy bones.

- *Forcing propulsion.* Provide children with foam javelins, beanbags and balls to hurl with varying degrees of force against walls or across open spaces.

Wonderful Ways to Move

Movement is an integral and natural part of being a human being; it helps us to feel alive. Young children just love to move and should be encouraged to do so whenever possible.

- *Stability mime.* Get children to pretend to be a mime, playing the role of a strongman/woman – lifting weights, flexing their muscles and pushing and pulling 'heavy boulders' from place to place.

- *Animal actions.* Develop locomotion movements by getting the children to move like horses (galloping), kangaroos (bouncing), rabbits (hopping) and frogs (leaping). Consider the movements of smaller animals such as caterpillars (wriggling), snails (sliding) and bugs (jumping).

- *Good Old British Bulldog.* Use this classic playground game to give chasing, dodging, racing and sprinting movements a context and purpose.

- *Gyming it.* Recreate movements made by people in the gym in the outdoor play area: walking, running, jogging, stretching and cycling.

- *Ball skills.* The children can use different-sized balls to practise kicking, volleying, striking, rolling and dribbling actions through adult-led and child-initiated activities.

- *'You can touch this.'* Support children in using their hands not only to throw but also to catch, bounce, hurl and dribble using balls and other resources including foam building blocks, beanbags and hoops.

- *Professionals in action.* Similar to 'Animal actions' (see above), but consider asking the children to move in the style of different occupations such as soldiers, conductors, footballers, climbers, wrestlers, dancers, swimmers and acrobats. Work to break down gender stereotyping by inviting children to move like Bat*girl*, *Darren* the Explorer, Super*girl* and Prince Bar-*na*-bie.

Resources to Support Movement

While the importance of quality planning, teaching and assessment cannot be overestimated, every good practitioner appreciates that resources play an important part in supporting children's progress in physical development. Do remember, though, that it is more about having the right *type* of resources to ensure high-quality provision as opposed to the quantity of resources available for use.

● *Doing a wheelie.* Where possible, provide a range of different-sized scooters, trikes, pedal and push bikes, cars, and trucks. Exciting additions include rickshaws, wagons, go-karts, sidecar trikes, step-on trikes, taxis and hand-propelled buggies.

● *Climbing high.* Plan for children to access ladders, scrambling nets, monkey runs, frames, crawler ramps and steps to strengthen arm and leg muscles.

● *Hands and knees.* Encourage children to move between high and low levels by setting up tunnels in criss-cross, wiggly and random layouts as part of an obstacle course.

● *Boooiiinnng!* Trampolines support intense physical development, balance and motor skills, and come in various sizes to suit the size of children and the setting. Consider investing in one.

● *Getting the balance just right.* Offer children a wealth of balance beams, boards, stepping stones, stairs, logs and tiles so they can find their centre.

● *Marvellous mats.* Assure children's safety and quality of movement by providing them with access to mats of different textures, thickness and shape appropriate to the children's age and the activity being undertaken.

● *Swing low, sweet chariot.* Build confidence and strength by encouraging children to swing from ropes, bars and high ladders.

● *Back and forth.* Promote swaying movements with rocking boats, chairs, rockers and see-saws.

Excellent Environments and Super Spaces

Access to the 'right places' for physical activity for young children is essential; they should be not only stimulating and well planned but also safe and secure. By making effective use of the wealth of different places available in the locality, children's physical development will be constantly challenged and enriched, thus encouraging progress and attainment.

- *The park.* Use the various pieces of equipment available to develop children's strength and confidence on stationary and moving apparatus.

- *The garden.* Encourage children to play outside in their back gardens with parents and carers, kicking balls and chasing each other.

- *The classroom.* Use carpeted zones, role-play areas and table-top activities to promote both fine and gross motor activity.

- *The school hall.* Utilize a weekly timetabled slot in 'big school' to help children develop a sense of space and appreciate the need for rules when working in this area.

- *The outdoor play area.* Provide plenty of access during sessions for children to utilize this space, giving them time to simply let off steam. Support them in practically experiencing changes to their body during physical activity while moving with controlled effort.

- *The local sports centre.* Work in partnership with designated personnel so that your children have the opportunity to use the multitude of facilities the centre has to offer.

- *After-school clubs.* Actively encourage older children in EYFS to attend clubs that promote physical activity, such as football, music and movement, and karate.

- *Any others?* Local playgrounds, secondary schools, nearby woods, the streets (for walking), playing fields and activity centres are other possibilities. How often are they accessed by your children? How could you promote them in your setting?

IDEA

15

Managing Physical and Personal Space

As a key strand of Learning and Development, children need ultimately to 'show awareness of space, of themselves and of others' (ELG). It takes time for children to judge body space effectively and develop an understanding of what personal space is, but this Idea is all about developing this ability a little more quickly.

- *The route to role play.* The children can use role-play activities to create pathways. For example, they could devise different ways to navigate through the indoor setting to 'Grandma's house' as Little Red Riding Hood.

- *Blanket space.* Get children to create their own space using a blanket, for example a sitting space (picnic blanket), a hiding space (den), a sleeping space (tent) or an imaginary space (seaside – with a blanket to represent the sea).

- *Group games.* Encourage children to join in with whole-group games that involve following or imitating others to develop control and coordination over body movements. Examples include Follow My Leader, Copy Cats and Follow Me Up.

- *Carpet squares.* Purchase carpet offcuts, giving one to each child to sit on so that they appreciate the concept of personal space. Alternative ideas include using hoops, spots and chalk crosses on the floor.

- *Share, share, share.* Encourage games and activities that involve the children in sharing resources with other children. Examples include sharing out tokens to use the trikes, playing giant Yahtzee and passing sand timers to the next child in the 'wagon' queue.

- *Bodies a-bobbing.* Through physical activity, such as having the children wash the practitioner's car or dance at the 'local disco', instigate and support discussions about body parts and ways of moving.

- *Sing out loud and proud.* Engage children in singing action songs ('Head, Shoulders, Knees and Toes', for example) to promote movement and coordination skills.

IDEA 16

Moving without Equipment

The great thing about movement is that most children need only one thing to help them: their bodies. Practitioners should ensure that babies and young children engage in lots of different ways of moving with just their body, and visual imagery is a wonderful way to achieve this.

- *'We're going on a . . . [bear] hunt.'* Adapt the well-known story by hunting for a squirrel, treasure, a friend, a book, a magician or a DVD, moving through real and imaginary spaces while adding vocal sound effects such as 'Oh, oh! Trees! Tall, broad trees! Scramble, scramble, SNAP! SNAP!' (twig breaking).

- *Modern-day mulberry bush.* Teach the first verse of the famous rhyme 'Here We Go Round the Mulberry Bush' and then invent a verse of your own, linking it to movements applicable to different situations such as housework, playing sports, gardening and playing different musical instruments.

- *Quality challenges.* Stress movement qualities – fast/slow, heavy/light, straight/curved – through 'Can you . . . ?' tasks. Examples include 'Can you move like a snail? An arrow? A car? A gentle raindrop falling? A tall tree? A doughnut?' Other suggestions include 'Can you move as if your feet are stuck in treacle? Like a spinning top? A kite? A "pinged" rubber band? Popping bubbles?'

- *Beans beanz beens.* This is a wonderful game with plenty of possibilities. Ask children to move in response to types of beans called out by the practitioner, such as chilli beans (shake shoulders), jumping beans, runner beans, beans on toast (curl up in a ball), broad beans (arms and legs out).

- *Traditional tales.* Bring stories alive through exaggerated mime – for example, 'The Enormous Turnip', 'Cinderella' or 'Jack and the Beanstalk'.

Linking Songs and Movement Together

One of the most effective ways to develop children's movements is by putting the movements into a context. Learning and singing songs is good practice in the early years, and so by combining songs – the right songs – and movement, practitioners are able to help children's physical development. A wealth of classic suggestions is provided below for you or your children to select from:

- Head, Shoulders, Knees and Toes
- Here We Go Round the Mulberry Bush
- If You're Happy and You Know It
- One Finger, One Thumb, Keep Moving
- Peter Hammers with One Hammer
- Simon Says
- Ring-a-Ring-a-Roses
- Follow My Leader
- The Wheels on the Bus
- The Farmer's in His Den
- Miss Polly Had a Dolly
- I'm a Little Teapot
- Incy Wincy Spider
- Twinkle, Twinkle Little Star
- Jack and Jill
- Polly Put the Kettle On
- Who Stole the Cookies from the Cookie Jar?
- Five Little Sausages
- Ten in the Bed
- Old MacDonald Had a Farm
- Pop Goes the Weasel!
- The Hokey Cokey.

Promoting Rough-and-Tumble Play

A number of practitioners may disregard this Idea on the grounds of not wanting the children they work with to get hurt. Indeed, rough-and-tumble (R&T) involves kicking, chasing, tumbling and rolling, wrestling, and grappling movements. However, this is a very common type of play in both sexes (though more so in boys) and it has many physical benefits for children who engage in it.

- *Play fighting versus real fighting.* Look for the 'play face', the lack of contact from 'apparent' kicks and blows, and the turn taking to be chased or 'duffed up'; these signs indicate it is a play fight. If you see the opposite to the above, then it is a real fight.

- *Superhero play.* Superheroes of both genders (think X-Men and the Fantastic Four) fight the baddies to save the day. Have a collection of superhero and baddy capes, masks and costumes available to encourage this kind of physical play.

- *Hiy Yah!* Children may simply be recreating movements they have learned at their karate, judo or kung fu classes. Use this as an opportunity to encourage others to join clubs or invite class leaders to come and talk to the children in the setting about their wonderful skills in movement.

- *Father and son.* Many fathers play R&T with their sons as a way of bonding with them. Suggest this as 'weekend play' for dads and lads to get their heart rates up, their legs working and their excess energy burned!

- *Wrestling ring.* Rope off a space outside on a soft surface where children can have a pretend wrestling match under close supervision.

Building Sequences of Movement

A progressive element of Movement and Space is for children to develop 'combinations' of different movements that can be repeated as and when necessary. With repetitive practice and a little creativity, children are likely to be able to perform movements with increased control and coordination. But how can practitioners support children in this kind of progression?

● *Story time.* Use adapted stories as a resource in helping children to build sequences of movement – for example, the Gruffalo leaping, skipping, hopping and jumping through the woods.

● *Movements of the services.* Work with the children to build movement sequences based on the actions of police officers, firefighters and soldiers, including crawling, pulling and rolling.

● *Sequence cards.* Allow children to select a number of photographs of babies and children performing simple movements such as twisting, turning, jumping, stopping and running. Put the cards into a sequence, asking them to perform it in order.

● *Obstacle courses.* Provide a selection of different resources for babies and children to access and build courses with, encouraging them to navigate their way through them in different ways. Add or remove challenges depending on the needs and abilities of particular children.

● *Sing a song of movement.* Make up songs that encourage children to perform movements on either a random or a progressively repetitive basis – for example (to the tune of 'Sing a Rainbow'), 'Run and twizzle and flick and spring, / Gallop and sidestep it too. / I can move my body, move my body, / Move it just like you.'

● *One's easy, five's hard.* Play a game whereby you call out a way of moving, labelling it 'one' and then add another way to the sequence – for example, One = Jump! Two = Hop! Three = Crouch down! The more numbers you add, the more movements the children have to remember; the quicker they are said out loud, the harder it gets.

Activities and Games from the PE Store 2

Here is another selection of activities to breathe new life into your physical development provision in your setting. Enjoy (hopefully not only the children but also you)!

- *Cor! Conkers!* Teach children to play this traditional 'schoolboy' pastime, allowing them to prepare the conkers with children-friendly drills.

- *Whisk away.* Set up the water tray with rotary whisks and a mild shampoo or bubble bath. Work those arm muscles by challenging the children to create a bubble mountain for the 'Bubble Beast' to live on.

- *'Come on and Do the Conga.'* Legally download a copy of 'Come on and Do the Conga' by Black Lace, teaching the children how to move in the line while holding on to someone else's waist. Begin with small lines of children, building these up as the children gain in confidence and ability. Alternatively, you might like to try their other 'moving' classic, 'Agadoo'.

- *Musical statues 'in action'.* Play this classic party game but ask the children to freeze as a 'sports' statue in mid-movement – for example, as a footballer kicking a football, a cricketer bowling or a rugby player throwing a rugby ball.

- *Rocking Robin.* Sing well-known rhymes such as 'See-saw, Margery Daw' or 'Row, Row, Row Your Boat' as the children engage with spring-activated or child-operated see-saws or sit-on rockers.

- *Alphabet actions* Use the poem 'Alphabet Actions' by Tony Mitton or make up your own version of the poem with the children to promote gross and fine motor movements – for example, 'A is for an ant scurrying home for his tea, / B is a bat flapping his wings; he's after me! . . . '

Section 3:
Investigating Healthy
and Bodily Awareness

The Value of Rest

Do you take moments of rest when you attend the gym or undertake household chores? As with adults, young children need to appreciate the importance of rest in their lives, and practitioners should remain mindful of this Idea by ensuring that children get enough of it during each day.

- *Take a breather.* Encourage children who are engaging in physically energetic play to actively take a moment's rest to recharge the batteries and catch their breath. Model this wherever possible.

- *Badly behaved?* Observe children to see how their behaviour changes as they get tired. Take note of this and respond with suggestions of having a bit of 'chill-out time' to pre-empt issues where appropriate.

- *Rest areas.* Work with the children to create a rest area that they can access as and when they wish. See Idea 22 for resource suggestions to include in these areas.

- *Put rest on the timetable.* Provide moments of rest for babies and children as part of the daily provision, perhaps at carpet time, after outdoor play, during story time and at snack time.

- *Game play.* Play simple games that encourage children to have moments of rest. Possibilities include musical statues (stillness) and musical bumps (sitting down).

- *Restful activities.* Provide activities that encourage children to be calm and restful. For example, they could read books to Teddy in the book corner, paint in response to lullaby music, eat a snack, complete a jigsaw or perform yoga (see www.yogaforchildren.co.uk).

IDEA
22

The Importance of Sleep

Research indicates that children all over the world go to settings every day deprived of the recommended age-related hours of sleep (NHLBI, 2008). This has a real impact on children's abilities to listen, learn and behave. We need, therefore, to provide time to support children in understanding how sleep promotes good health.

- *Have a snooze.* Provide babies and children with blankets, cushions, pillows, sleeping bags, duvets and/or teddy bears so that they can 'rest their eyes' during the day, as and where appropriate.

- *Rest mats.* A number of settings have introduced 'rest mats' (similar to exercise mats) for their children, on which they can lie down, power-nap, doze or just take time to chill out.

- *Good old Personal, Health, Social and Citizenship Education (PHSCE) and circle time.* Use these opportunities to talk to the children about the need for sleep and how they can get a good night's sleep by devising a bedtime routine. Alternatively, work together to formulate a simple series of bedtime dos and don'ts. See www.kidshealth.org/kid/stay_healthy/body/not_tired.html, 'How to Catch your ZZZs', for ideas.

- *Zzzzzzz in the home corner.* Set up a 'bedroom' in the role-play area with the children so that they can engage in purposeful 'snooze' play. Include storybooks, pyjamas, slippers, 'Wee Willy Winkie' hats, sleep masks and soft music on tape/CD to enrich activity.

- *Interesting internet.* Visit www.sleepforkids.org, www.raisingkids.co.uk or www.helpguide.org to support children's, parents' and your own understanding of the importance of sleep.

For further information on the research work of the NHLBI, see www.nhlbi.nih.gov/about/ncsdr.

The Need for Water

An essential part of being healthy and active is being adequately hydrated. Even though water is the most important nutrient in the living world, and is a vital component of our diets to support growth and body maintenance, many children (and adults) are not consuming nearly enough. So what can practitioners do about it?

● *Fabulous foods*. Work to ensure children have daily opportunities to eat types of fruit and vegetables that have a high water content, such as watermelon and oranges.

● *Types of water*. Provide children with different types of water – tap, natural, mineral, bottled, spring, purified, those processed with health claims – for them to sample and compare.

● *A wealth of water bottles*. Good practice recommends that practitioners provide children with individually labelled water bottles to access throughout the day. An alternative is water jugs with individually named plastic cups.

● *Water fountain*. Many settings are adopting the international practice of installing water fountains to ensure that children have access to fresh cold water.

● *Talk about it*. Plan opportunities to talk to the children about why they need water, especially in the summer months. Make them aware of how they lose water through visiting the toilet, respiration and sweating, and how this water needs to be replaced.

● *Water with razzmatazz*. Some young children do not like the taste of water, so support them in adding flavourings such as lemon, lime, cordial (for example, orange or strawberry) or food colourings to spice it up a bit.

● *Say it with a poster*. Purchase or design posters with the children that have positive images and slogans concerning water, which will encourage them to have a good gulp of H_2O.

● *Wet your whistle*. If you encourage children to drink water, show them how much water *you* are drinking as well. Carry a bottle of water around as you play, so they can see the water level falling.

IDEA 24

Food, Glorious Food!

Healthy and *balanced* are two key words that underpin the kind of diet recommended for parents, carers and practitioners to provide for young children to help ensure a healthy lifestyle for them. Ways in which this can be achieved have been developed in response to recommendations from the Food Standards Agency (see www.eatwell.gov.uk).

- *Let them enjoy what they eat.* Younger children need more calcium and fat in their diets, so please do not make them feel guilty for eating chocolate or cakes. These foods are good for them as long as they are eaten in moderation in relation to the rest of their diet.

- *Various varieties.* Children need fruit and vegetables but these should not always be apples and carrots. Keep visual records of the foods you offer to children to avoid unnecessary repetition. For example, you could create a fruit board or fasten plastic foods to a mobile.

- *Ample amounts.* Toddlers are able to eat the same amount of food as an adult but cannot consume it all in one sitting. Provide small snacks throughout the day to maintain energy levels.

- *Starched and fibred up.* Offer children sandwiches made up of one thick slice of white bread and one of wholegrain. At the 'Breakfast Club' role-play area, invite children to try porridge along with other cereals.

- *'Get yer fruit and veg 'ere!'* Provide children with a selection of fresh, frozen, tinned, dried and juiced fruit and vegetables. Offer fruit juices as an alternative to water and milk. Put chopped bananas on sandwiches instead of having banana pieces on their own in a bowl.

- *Keep the fat low.* Work to ensure that unsaturated fats *are* part of the foods children consume by putting seeds, nuts, sunflower spreads (instead of butter) and avocados on the 'menu'. Do consider those children with nut allergies.

- *Sweet sugar. Do* offer sugary drinks and sweets to children, but infrequently. Again, use a food log to see how often you are offering them.

Supporting Young Children's Eating Habits

Practitioners and settings play an important and influential role in encouraging babies and young children to develop healthy eating habits. With the support of other children, adults, and parents and carers, practitioners are likely to establish and embed thinking and behaviours that, hopefully, will last a lifetime.

- *Get them to prepare it.* Children are more likely to try new foods if they are involved in its preparation. Preparing food will help them to understand recommended hygienic practices and develop important fine motor skills as well.

- *Sit and eat.* Avoid rushing around at snack time, passing plates of food about and putting straws in cartons of milk. Sit and talk with the children, consuming some of the food and drink on offer. If you do not eat it, the children might wonder what is wrong with it.

- *Splendid speech.* Make snack time a sociable time by talking about 'grub', their likes and dislikes, and the texture, colour and smell of different foods. Build children's confidence in trying new and unusual foods through praise, encouragement and prompting.

- *Variety is the spice of life.* Prepare snacks in different ways to make snack time exciting and adventurous. Try slicing and grating carrots, and providing dried raisins and grapes.

IDEA

26

Eating and Drinking Inside and Outside

Many settings allow children to consume foods and liquids indoors only, as food hygiene and health and safety considerations dominate practitioners' thinking. We should, however, consider ways in which we can offer children food and drink irrespective of whether they are inside or outside.

- *Teddy bears' picnic.* Regularly lay a series of blankets outside that children can sit on and eat their snack with a selection of teddy bears.

- *Running water.* Purchase a number of runners' hand-held easy-grip sports bottles that the children can fill with water and run around with.

- *Le petit café.* Set up a small table with chairs and a tablecloth near to where food and drink are kept outside. Suggest that children have their snack there, inviting individuals to play waiter/waitress.

- *Keep it cool and safe.* Keep milk and juices in a cooler box so that they are nicely chilled for children to consume. Protect prepared snacks and fruit in durable plastic containers that can be easily opened and closed by the children themselves.

- *Selected seating.* Designate certain chairs, benches or areas for children to use to have their snack. Use labels and pictures to clarify their use.

- *Caretaking duties.* Provide children with plastic gloves, asking them to help you tie up and dispose of bin bags around the setting to prevent unpleasant smells and avoid attracting flies.

Body Hygiene

Teaching young children ways to ensure good personal hygiene is regarded as the best way not only to prevent the spread of infection and disorders but also to keep them healthy in their later life. To embed a concern for hygiene as standard practice, practitioners are recommended to try any or all of the following:

- *Wishy-washy day*. Set up a launderette role-play area with real children's clothing to wash and dry, to teach about the importance of having clean clothes. Provide rubber gloves to protect hands from the soap suds.

- *Put a sock in it*. Encourage children to wear socks when wearing trainers or shoes so that the insides of their footwear do not smell or get dirty.

- *Cardboard combs*. Teach children about looking after their hair by cutting out wide-toothed cardboard combs for them to pull through their own locks. Avoid using real combs in case children catch or pass on nits.

- *Ting teeth*. Allow children to swill water around their mouth during the day to prevent food sticking to or in between their pearly whites.

- *Have you washed your hands?* Make up little chants and rhymes with the children to remind them to wash their hands before they have something to eat or drink. 'Have you all washed your hands, kids?' Reply: 'YES, WE HAVE!'

- *Oh pants!* Create a 'timeline' with the days of the week, selecting which underwear and socks or tights Tina (doll) or Max (Action Man) should wear each day to promote an understanding of the need for daily changing of undergarments.

Clothing and Hygiene

For children to be able to take part fully in physical activity, it is important that they be dressed appropriately. Practitioners need to be aware of cultural considerations – hair, footwear, jewellery, hijabs and turbans – that may affect what children wear. Also, settings need to ensure they have appropriate policies and assessments to ensure they are protected if children are hurt.

- *Sporty people.* Show children images of different sportspeople. What are they wearing? Does any of the clothing have specialized names? Why are they wearing them? How is the male clothing different to the female's? How is the clothing different for various sports? Why? Compare and contrast ideas.

- *Phew! Smelly!* Show children real examples of sportswear and ask them to consider what will happen to them when they are being worn by people who are being physically active. What should happen to the clothing? Why?

- *Sports centre role play.* Create an outdoor role-play area where children can play tennis, badminton, football and cricket. Provide play clothes for them to wear, encouraging them to throw them in the 'dirty' basket once they have finished their game.

- *Soap and suds.* Imagine that the hare and the tortoise have left their sports clothing to be washed. Invite individuals to put on some rubber gloves and wash and dry them out before their next race.

- *Keeping clothing clean.* Provide children with sweat bands, flannels, towels and wipes to get rid of unwanted perspiration when engaging in 'puff and pant' physical activity.

Recognizing Changes to the Body during and after Physical Activity

Many forms of physical activity bring about some sort of effect on the body. Children should be encouraged to recognize these effects by comparing their bodies prior to being active and after being active. Consider integrating these suggestions into your day-to-day practice so that children appreciate that these changes are the *result* of engaging in physical activity.

- *Boom-diddy-boom-diddy-boom.* Encourage children to feel their heart rate prior to and after a period of energetic activity. Show them where they can feel their heart beat on their chest or teach them how to take their pulse in their wrists or neck (remember: no thumbs).

- *Talking through music.* Have a selection of musical instruments to hand for children to use to represent how parts of their bodies have changed after enthusiastic periods of movement. For example, the fast beating of a drum could indicate rapid breathing.

- *Technical testers.* Use simple electronic thermometers and pulse monitors to show children how their body temperature and heart rate increase during physical activity. What happens to these readings when their bodies cool down?

- *Damp factor.* Show children how their bodies sweat when engaged in physical activity by asking them to dab a piece of paper towel on the back of their hand or brow. Talk sensitively about how our bodies react to exercise in different ways.

- *Hot/fast stuff.* Ask children to put their hand in front of their mouth to feel their breath during and after physical activity. Does it get hotter and faster? Why?

IDEA 30

Awareness of Cultural Differences and Considerations

Many settings and practitioners strive to ensure that the traditions, beliefs and practices of children belonging to different cultures are embraced and positively integrated into their day-to-day practice. Integrating these into learning and teaching is an important consideration to ensure equality and effective practice in all early years settings.

- *Forbidden foods*. In some cultures, the consumption of certain foods and drinks, such as pork or coffee, is prohibited. Work to ensure you are aware of those foods and drinks children are not able to have, considering appropriate alternatives.

- *Fasting*. A number of faiths encourage or expect their followers to fast for certain periods of time. It is inappropriate to plan for long periods of energetic physical activity for children during this time, so consider preparing fine motor activities as an alternative.

- *Jewellery*. Many young children wear cultural jewellery, and practitioners need to speak sensitively with parents and carers to make them aware of the potential dangers of wearing this during physical activity, not only to their own child but also to other children in the setting. Use waist bands and surgical tape as a way of covering jewellery that is not to be removed.

- *Clothing*. Some children, particularly girls, need to cover certain parts of their bodies. While practitioners and settings are keen to get children to wear T-shirts and shorts, there is no reason why all children should not have the option to wear tracksuits or churidar trousers.

- *Toilet training*. Be mindful of the fact that in some cultures boys are used to sitting on the toilet as opposed to standing. Talk with parents and carers to establish the right practice for individual children.

Section 4:
Using Equipment
and Materials

Tremendous Tools

Children need to have regular access to a range of different tools so that their progress linked to Using Equipment and Materials is assured, particularly with regard to fine motor development. The idea of trying to use these tools in creative ways drives the suggestions made below to maintain interest and develop skills.

- *Chore tools.* Provide different tools so that children are able to help you undertake 'jobs' in and around the setting, such as weeding the vegetable patch with rakes and trowels, and sweeping the sand up using a hand-held dustpan and brush.

- *Messy tools.* Allow children to select from an array of sticks, rollers, moulds, cutters, modelling tools and utensils when playing with dough, sand, clay or plasticine.

- *Home corner tools.* Encourage children to use different utensils for eating and cooking in both role-play and real-life situations. Broaden experiences by providing chopsticks, ice cream scoops and pizza cutters.

- *Squeeze-me tools.* Support children in using tools that require a pump action to operate, such as hole-punches, snips, tweezers and scissors, thus creating the desired effect of improving their motor skills.

- *Building tools.* Break down gender stereotypes by providing coloured hammers (both plastic and wooden), saws and screwdrivers for DIY and construction play.

- *Writing tools.* Give children access to various writing implements throughout the entire setting, including chunky felt-tip pens, chalk, fountain pens, ballpoint pens that light up, wax crayons, pastels and pencils.

- *ICT tools.* Consider the value of keyboards with different-sized keys, programmable robots, musical units, videos and cameras in developing fine motor skills.

- *Sewing tools.* Supervise the use of metal and plastic needles when planning for threading and creative activities.

- *Creative tools.* Paintbrushes are an essential tool for the early years. Rollers, printing blocks, stamps and clay tools offer a wealth of creative possibilities, too.

Clever Construction Kits

The place, purpose and use of construction kits in early years settings are wonderfully multifaceted. Kits have the potential, for example, to promote problem solving, design, balance and creative skills. More importantly, they are valuable in supporting the manipulative and fine motor management skills of children who come into contact with them.

- *Bricks to build with.* Provide children with small building bricks that can be interlinked, such as Duplo and Sticklebricks, to develop capabilities of managing pressure and force judgements. Large building blocks (pretend house bricks, Featherlite bricks) are useful in utilizing gross motor skills.

- *Tactile-tastic.* Large, brightly coloured pieces of construction, such as Popoids heads, are valuable in supporting babies to mouth items, thus developing body, space and distance awareness.

- *Moving kits.* Kits with moving parts, such as wheels, axles or turntables – all found in Mobilo – are valuable for developing skills, particularly if children have made a car that they wish to send to their friend. Judgement of direction, a sense of timing to release the car from their fingers, and how much force they need to send it all come into play in this activity.

- *Star skills.* Construction toys that encourage children to hold, grasp and grip objects and tools are strongly recommended. Examples include Interstar, Technico and the Brio Builder range, which develop skills on different levels.

- *Pincer-grip it.* Children continue to develop this intricate finger–thumb management well into their third year. Kits such as Kid K'nex and Cleversticks work well to address this.

To view or order any of the kits recommended, contact TTS Group on 0800 318 686 or visit www.tts-group.co.uk.

Marvellously Malleable Materials

Good early years practice advocates that children learn through their senses, and there is nothing more sensory than malleable materials. So, roll up your sleeves (and the children's) and prepare to get messy.

- *Super slime.* Explore the properties of slime (three cups of soap flakes whisked into 1 litre of warm water with food colouring) with fingers, scoops and sticks.

- *Mucky mud pies.* Put peat-free compost in water, encouraging the children to mix it up and mould it into pies with their hands.

- *Textured dough.* Prepare dough (200g of plain flour, 1 tablespoon of vegetable oil, 100g of salt, 300ml of water, 2 tablespoons of tartar mixed in a saucepan on a low heat until softly textured), adding food colourings as appropriate, along with poppy seeds, lentils or rice to stimulate those touch receptors.

- *Peculiar plasticine.* Pull, push, flatten and shape this versatile material into different objects, including 2D and 3D shapes, objects, numbers and letters of various sizes.

- *Slippery shaving foam.* Supervise children squeezing shaving foam from the can into a low tray, suggesting they draw in the foam, along with rubbing it between their fingers and squeezing it.

- *Clever clay.* Make balls of clay and aprons available so that the children can pummel, poke and roll it using artists' tools.

- *Classic cornflour.* No setting is complete without having a cornflour tray (cornflour and water) along with children covered from head to toe in cornflour!

- *Smelly salt dough.* Make salt dough with the children (see www.gigglemoose.com/salt_dough_recipe.htm), adding a selection of scents, such as curry powder, herbs and fruit oils, to get those nasal receptors working.

IDEA 34

Health and Safety Considerations

Engaging with any form of equipment or materials brings with it health and safety risks that need to be monitored and managed to the best of practitioners' abilities. This is not to say that children should not be taught how to use equipment and materials safely; in fact, the first suggestion supports this idea.

- *Look at me! Look at me!* Work in role as a child, using scissors, bats and dough in inappropriate ways. Can children identify what you are doing wrong and what you should be doing? What would happen if everyone behaved like that with these resources? How do practitioners deal with incidences like this? Ask the children to show you.

- *Safe storage.* Use labelled boxes, trays and holders to ensure that equipment is not stored unnecessarily together. For examples, place bats and balls in separate containers so that children do not get hurt when they try to access them at the start of a session.

- *Safe snips.* Put plasticine around the tips of blades of scissors if stored in milk cartons to save fingers from getting cut when locating a pair for cutting and sticking activities.

- *Safety rules.* Make learning and teaching about health and safety an integral part of planning and delivering activities. For example, when painting, the rule is nil by mouth! When playing on the bikes, children should be taught to avoid running on to the 'racing track' when vehicles are on the move.

- *Posters and pictures.* Display, around activities or around the setting as a whole, images of children working safely with equipment and materials as a visual reminder of expected behaviours.

Sensory Equipment and Materials

Children in the first few years of their physical development need constant stimulation, and one of the ways that this can be achieved is through stimulation of the senses. Many consider this kind of practice suitable only for children with special educational needs, but mainstream children will benefit greatly from experiences that heighten their sensory awareness:

- *Touch it*. Provide balls with textured surfaces. Offer children access to different surfaces to move on, such as grass, gravel, tarmac, wood, bark, leaves, sand and stones.

- *Taste it*. Stimulating children's taste buds can only really be achieved through offering different food types to children through snack and meal times. Set up tasting booths for the children to sample new and exotic foods. Allow children to prepare food in different ways, evaluating which they like the best by the way it tastes.

- *Smell it*. Grate scented candles into sealed pots with small holes in the top to stimulate nasal receptors. Purchase plug-in odorizers to add freshness to the air. Raise awareness of health and safety issues when thinking about smells: smoke from a fire, medicine bottles, vapours from a leaking gas cooker.

- *Hear it*. Support children when catching balls by providing them with inflatable balls that have small balls or bells inside them so that they make a sound when thrown through the air. Objects that squeak amuse children, while household toys such as vacuum cleaners and lawnmowers make noise with a purpose.

- *See it*. Vary the kind of resources available for children. Big, bright and bold equipment made from plastic is visually appealing, but consider purchasing resources made of wood and other natural materials.

Fine Motor Madness

Developing children's fine motor skills is an essential part of physical development and should continue well into Key Stage 1/2. This, like many aspects of Learning and Development, can be potentially heavily resource-laden, and practitioners are encouraged to ensure they provide a wide range of opportunities to put these resources into meaningful contexts.

- *Flippy-flappy.* Set up a book area with different texts containing flaps, tabs and movable parts. Work with children to make a class book that incorporates these features.

- *Fine motor mat.* Purchase a large piece of fabric and stitch to it large zips, Velcro straps, pockets with buttons, press studs, pull cords and laces. Lay it out on the floor and allow the children to master control over these fiddly features.

- *Snack time.* Prepare a snack but encourage children to come and collect it themselves. Encourage them to hold plates, use spoons, pour drinks and use fingers to eat with.

- *Great gardening.* Build up children's control and manipulation of tools by asking for their help in digging the soil, watering the plants, weeding the ground and tidying the edges. Provide them with small gardening gloves. Can they put them on by themselves?

- *Musical madness.* Offer opportunities for babies and young children to play freely with a selection of musical instruments that encourage banging, plucking, twisting, shaking and flicking actions.

- *Slice and dice.* Use cooking role play as a vehicle for children to work with various tools, building up skills, movements and control over whisks, ladles and spatulas.

Left, Right or Ambidextrous?

Interestingly, one person in every ten is left-handed; boys are one and a half times more likely to be left-handed than girls. It is important for practitioners to be mindful of this so that they are able to support those who are 'lefties' or even ambidextrous through their provision and practice in the setting.

- *Encourage it*. If you see young children reaching for, throwing, pointing or catching objects with one particular hand, then praise them. Being left-handed simply means having a dominant right side of the brain. Changing this is very difficult, so please don't try.

- *Mirror teaching*. Right-handed practitioners are encouraged to avoid sitting next to or behind a child who is left-handed when trying to teach them, for example, how to hold and use a fork. Instead, sit *opposite* the child so that they see the hand movements in the proper direction – that is, the mirror image. The same goes for left-handed practitioners working with right-handed children.

- *Right/left resources*. Take care in labelling left-handed children as 'clumsy'. Although they may appear awkward using tools, this may be simply because the tools are not appropriate for them. For example, scissors may be right-handed, and the computer mouse may be placed on the right-hand side of the monitor. Purchase left-handed equipment – pencil sharpeners, pens and pencil grips, kitchen utensils and musical instruments – clearly marking it for left-handed use only.

- *Wonderful website*. Visit www.lefthandedchildren.org for advice, ideas and information to support children, parents and carers, and practitioners.

IDEA
38

Building Muscle Strength in the Hands and Arms

For children to be able to show increasing skill at manipulating, and increasing control over equipment and materials, it is essential that they have opportunities to build up their strength in their hands and arms. While this does not mean we want all our children to have 'Popeye' biceps, we do need to think of ways to promote the idea of toning and developing their muscles.

- *Climb to the top.* Encourage children to climb up ladders, ropes and wall bars using imaginative 'firefighter/gymnast/superhero' play as an incentive.

- *Setting up and clearing away.* Organize children in groups to help carry boxes of equipment, chairs and mats into and out of the outdoor play area. Teach them effective ways to grip, lift, lower and position themselves around objects in order to 'share the load'.

- *Pump it up.* Provide children with stress balls or other squeezable resources that can be used to build muscles in the hands and arms.

- *Swing while you're winning.* Provide opportunities for children to swing from monkey bars, platforms or climbing frames in the outdoor play area or at the local park to build muscle strength in their hands and arms.

- *Getting parents in on the act.* Encourage parents and carers to take their children swimming as this is a wonderful way to build children's water confidence and strengthen their arm muscles as they attempt different strokes. Under-5s tennis, golf and basketball clubs are other powerful alternatives.

Physical Activity with an International Flavour

Physical movement is a universal activity. Practitioners are encouraged to embrace ways in which young people in other countries 'move' so that children in their own settings have the opportunity to develop knowledge, skills and understanding that directly impact on the diverse ways in which their bodies can be active.

- *USA it*. How about a bit of American football, baseball or basketball? Adapting these games for young children to play is relatively easy. Think about the rules, the resources and the health and safety issues.

- *France it*. Have a *Tour de France* day with lots of cycling. Boules is a simple game that can be played with plastic balls filled with water with a little sand on the floor.

- *Spain it*. Get out the frilly dresses, some hard-soled shoes and some castanets from the music trolley and have fun teaching the children to flamenco-dance!

- *Down Under it*! A few black vests and a rugby ball may help little children to feel like the New Zealand All Blacks team.

- *China it*. Support children in engaging in badminton activities – serving, hitting and moving. Parents, carers or local experts may be able to introduce a few kung fu moves into children's movement repertoire as well.

- *Russia it*. Fold your arms, bend your knees and kick those legs out as the children engage in Russian gypsy folk dancing moves.

Other international activities include belly dancing, ice skating, judo, yoga, softball, volleyball, taekwondo, handball, tug-of-war, netball and hockey. Use the internet to find out how to play these and how they can be adapted for young children.

Activities and Games from the PE Store 3

Select from this third plethora of activities below to spice up your planning, your delivery and children's experiences.

- *Ball toss.* Organize the children into a small circle, either indoors or in a large, open area. A lightweight ball (a beach ball works very well) is then thrown into the mix of children, who are to try to keep hitting the ball into the air for as long as possible without it touching the ground. Can they build up the amount of time they can keep the ball going?

- *Walking blocks.* Make walking blocks out of wood and string so that the children can walk around with 'Herman Munster' shoes on!

- *ABCs and 1-2-3s.* Get children to use their bodies to form letters and number shapes, stretching and bending as needed. Talk about how they are manipulating their bodies. Can they collaborate with others to make larger versions of these symbols?

- *Gutter ball.* Get a safely prepared piece of guttering, place a plastic golf or table tennis ball in it and get two children, one at each end, to blow it. Who has the most 'puff' to blow it off the end?

- *Noodles galore.* Purchase colourful foam swimming-pool noodles for children to use as hurdles to leap over. Alternatively, use them as bats to hit balls or each other with (!), or pretend they are imaginary animals such as horses and bulls.

- *Pop! Pop! Pop!* Lay out large pieces of 'big bubble' bubble wrap on the floor and assign small groups of children – with no shoes or socks on – to burst as many bubbles as they can using different parts of their feet. Challenges using other body parts can also be made.

- *Inside skating.* Make 'ice skates' out of large, washed-out cardboard milk cartons, providing children with socks or the ends of tights to wear on their feet.

- *Building block bowling.* Create skittles out of towers of small wooden building blocks, using footballs (2- to 3-year-olds) or tennis balls (4- to 5-year-olds) to knock them over.

Section 5:
Challenges for
Physical Development

IDEA 41

When Should I Open the Doors? – timetabling for physical activity

A large number of settings ensure that physical development forms part of a 'balanced daily diet of provision' for children by opening the doors to the outdoor play area at certain times during the day or session. But is this enough? The following suggestions are designed to support the idea of maximizing the amount of physical activity that takes place in an already hectic timetable for young children.

- *Read the signs.* Young children will become restless, irritable and challenging if they are cooped up indoors for too long. Get them out when you can.

- *Block it.* Settle children into the setting initially by giving them access just to the indoor provision. Once all of the children have arrived, allow them to venture outside, adopting a free-flow approach between the two areas. Alternatively, consider allowing the children to access the outdoor play area as soon as they come into the setting. What's stopping you?

- *Timetable it inside.* Set up carpet areas or small open spaces inside the setting with CD music playing and scarves available, encouraging the children to 'move to the beat'.

- *As and when.* Raise physical activity levels by planning opportunities for movement, be it gross or fine. Examples include pouring water into cups, collecting aprons from the other side of the room, operating hole punches and stretching up high to reach books on a shelf.

- *Trips out.* Plan educational visits that promote physical movement, formulating timetables that require physical activity. Examples include walking to the park, running to the eating area, skipping over to the animal pen.

Taking the Indoors Outside and Bringing the Outside In

One of the biggest challenges for practitioners is appreciating that physical development does not simply take place *outside*; it is, or should be, an integral part of the practice that takes place *inside* the setting. The Idea of taking the indoors outside and bringing the outside in is designed to encourage practitioners to reflect on the potential of the space, and the resources, and the adults they have available.

- *Beam me up, Scotty.* Bring the balance beam inside and set it up on the carpeted area, allowing the children to play on it as part of an adult-led activity or a focused whole-group taught session. 'Who is going to have to walk the plank, Captain?'

- *Animal walks.* Take groups of children outside to 'walk' their partners, who model dog-, bear-, seal-, crab-, frog-, elephant- and rabbit-type movements.

- *Brilliant beanbags.* Develop skills linked to posture, balance and control inside by encouraging children to balance a beanbag on their heads, then on their feet as they move, then clamping it between their knees as they walk across the room to another activity.

- *Design and make in the open air.* Set up the traditionally 'only for indoors' junk modelling trolley outside so that children can practise their skills with scissors, hole punches and staplers in a new environment. Reiterate health and safety expectations – 'Do stand still when you have scissors in your hands' – and then allow the children to rise to the challenge of following these.

- *Rippling ribbons.* Move a number of tables to one side of the setting and allow the children to twist, turn and twizzle ribbons in an enclosed inside space, developing skills linked to control, spatial awareness and economy of movement.

Quality Outdoor Play Provision

Outdoor learning is an essential part of quality provision and practice in the EYFS, and practitioners and settings are constantly striving to ensure outdoor environments support not only physical development but the other areas of the early years curriculum as well. Ways in which babies and young children can engage in purposeful activities that promote physical skills include the following:

- *The bigger the better.* Allow regular access to swings, slides, see-saws, climbing frames and tunnels for large, gross motor movements.

- *Doing a wheelie.* Provide various 'wheeled' toys – bikes, trikes, carts, wheelbarrows, prams, buggies, cars and go-carts – that require children to steer, pedal, push and pull.

- *The littlies are the best.* Plan for frequent use of beanbags, balls, quoits, hoops, ropes and bats of different sizes, lengths and shapes so that children gain valuable experiences of hitting, kicking, throwing, chasing, catching, bouncing and jumping over small apparatus.

- *Follow the trail.* Use the outdoors to set up walks, trails, obstacle courses, circuits and treasure hunts that encourage children to move and navigate their way in, around, over, through and underneath resources and markings.

- *Great game play.* Play games that are better conducted outside, such as hide and seek, Ring-a-Ring-a-Roses songs, What's the Time, Mr Wolf? and Grandma's footsteps.

- *Yeah! The parachute!* Frequently air out the parachute, playing games with the children such as Cat and Mouse, Sharks, Sea Ripples and Mushroom Swap. See www.educationalexperience.co.nz/ezine/parachutegames.pdf for some excellent suggestions.

- *Don't forget the fine.* Always set up activities to promote fine motor skills. Suggestions include sand play, using knives and forks, doing jigsaws, threading beads and cutting up magazines with scissors.

Body Warmers

Many practitioners effectively prepare children for physical activity, particularly if they are using the indoor facilities such as the school hall. However, how many of us warm children up ready for their outdoor play activities? *No?* Well, let's adopt some good practice from this moment on, shall we?

- *Choose a movement.* Ask one child to select a movement from a choice of three, such as run, walk or skip. The children in the rest of the group must then perform this movement with confidence and capability.

- *Arms away.* Encourage children to make circles with their arms, moving them backwards and forwards, in alternate directions and across their chests.

- *Wiggling waists.* Get children to rotate their waists like a hula dancer, moving clockwise and anticlockwise (hands on hips are optional). Bend forwards, to the left and to the right, stretching the arms out where appropriate.

- *Frolicking feet.* Make the feet stamp, tiptoe, skip, hop, wiggle and slide, using different parts of the foot, such as heels, sides and toes.

- *Happy hands.* Encourage children to stretch their fingers out wide, wiggle them through their hair, clench their fists, clap, and 'fire' their fingers out of their closed hands – *whoosh!*

- *Legs, legs, legs.* Ask the children to sit on the floor, stretching out their legs while pointing their toes up, down and across the floor. Have them curl their legs under their bodies and then stretch their legs out wide like a pair of scissors.

- *Rotating wrists.* Spin the wrists clockwise, anticlockwise, down, up and side to side.

- *Bopping bodies.* Get the children to lie on their backs, shaking their arms, legs and heads. Put thumbs into armpits to create chicken movements. Rotate heads slowly to the left, right and down (never up).

Building Spaces in the Outdoor Area

One of the biggest difficulties practitioners face in providing children with opportunities for quality physical activity relates to the issue of space; there never seems to be enough of it, or what is available is rather limited. The following suggestions are designed to support the idea of maximizing the space available for the best possible provision.

- *Dig and build.* Have a 'digging' box (sand or soil) with a lid, on which can be put trays of construction materials for the children to build with.

- *Special seating.* Create a special seating area that can double up as an outdoor classroom and as a waiting area for parents and carers. This could also be a place for 'chilling out' between bursts of energetic play activity.

- *Diverse dividers.* Use boards, nets, curtains, cones and chalk markings to divide the space available into smaller, enclosed 'zones', thus enabling activities to be contained, and conducted safely.

- *Lots of logs.* Use log stumps not only as stepping stones but also as movable 'stools' for the children to sit on. Could the children build with them?

- *Fabulous fences.* Utilize the small spaces between the bars of the wire fences by hooking containers on to them. Large plastic milk bottles or buckets filled with resources for the children's play are suitable. Alternatively, tie long ribbons to the bars and encourage the children to develop their fine motor skills through 'outdoor weaving'.

- *Hiding holes.* Create spaces for children to hide in, for example by placing drapes over tables, or by having inflatable tents, boards leaning at an angle against walls, dens and cardboard boxes.

Drawing Out the Movement and Dance from Creative Development

From promoting a vocabulary to express movement – words such as 'marching', 'skipping' and 'jigging' – to developing spatial awareness and imagination, movement and dance is clearly of benefit for children's physical development. So, how can we raise the profile of Movement and Dance in our practice to maximize the potential of creative development in physical development?

- *Ring-a-ring-a games.* Play various traditional and cultural ring games (see www.geocities.com/traditions_uk/play for suggestions) to develop rhythmic movement and directional understanding.

- *Crash! Ting! Boom!* Provide children with a selection of musical instruments so that that they develop movements in response to the sounds they hear and make. For example, they could create star shapes to the 'Crash!', leap in the air to the 'Ting!' and curl up in a ball for the 'Boom!'.

- *Musical interludes.* Introduce musical extracts for children to move to as they build in confidence with the suggestion above, using music such as the 'Champagne Polka' by Strauss and *The Carnival of the Animals* by Saint-Saëns.

- *Motivate the movement.* Build up a collection of resources to encourage children to dance with, such as ribbons on sticks, scarves, streamers, wands, balloons and bubbles. Anything can be used; put in some wellies for the 'Puddle Dance'!

- *SLDs.* Model different ways of moving at different **S**peeds, **L**evels and **D**irections to enrich children's interpretation skills in relation to music and to other stimuli such as pictures, stories and songs.

- *Just the one, Mrs Wembley!* Perform movements initially limited to just one body part, progressing to fully exploring the potential for both gross and fine movements, such as the 'Arm Dance', the 'Leg Jig' (while sitting or lying on the floor) or the 'Shoulder Shrug'.

'Getting In on the Act' – practitioners and *their* involvement in Physical Development

It is so simple yet so effective: children are more likely to get involved in physical activity if they see practitioners having a go themselves. By acting as a positive and enthusiastic role model, you are in a wonderful position to draw young children into play-based learning and effectively support others in their own play. But how?

- *Look the part*. Wherever possible, dress appropriately for physical activity, swapping your shoes for trainers and working clothes for sports clothing to show you mean business.

- *You know you want to*. Pick up that bat and hit the ball. Unravel that rope and do ten skips. Push that pram around the play area while talking to the baby inside. If children see you doing it, they are likely to copy your actions and adopt them as part of their own play.

- *Show them your lunchbox*. When it is snack time or lunch time, allow children to see the foods and drinks you are consuming so that you practise what you preach in terms of eating healthy foods.

- *Ooze enthusiasm*. Allow children to see you enjoying physical activity through the way you use your voice, your facial expressions, your body movements, your choice of words and your encouragement of others. Try to keep those energy levels high as well.

- *Clubbing it*. Where possible, run or attend morning or after-school clubs for young children and their parents. Get experts in to support you, advertising local physical activities through noticeboards, leaflets, newsletters and conversations.

Battling against the Elements – the weather, outdoor provision and Physical Development

One of the biggest difficulties in providing access for children to the outdoor play area is the weather. Is it too wet? Is it too hot? It's quite windy – they might blow away! Changeable weather patterns make it difficult sometimes for practitioners to plan, set up, support learning and clear away outside without the weather interfering. So what can we do about this?

● *Wonderful wellies.* Provide children with wellington boots, plastic macs, hats, gloves and umbrellas and take them outside. Splashing and jumping in puddles is fun, good for gross motor skills, and building children's bone density.

● *Outfit no. 2.* Encourage parents and carers to bring a change of clothes for their child so that they can play in the snow, get wet and change or be changed into some dry clothes. Simple!

● *Wrap up warm.* Avoid depriving children of outdoor play just because it is cold and you do not want to stand in it. Get your thermals on, wear clothing to keep you warm and get outside.

● *Get moving.* Prevent getting cold by actively getting involved with the children's play; you will soon get warm.

● *See it as a bonus.* Take advantage of the weather by making and flying kites when it is windy, creating little shelters when it is raining and shady areas when it is sunny; all of which use gross and fine motor skills.

IDEA

49

Providing Enough Time for Movement

While educationalists, government reports and media coverage continually call for settings to dedicate more time to physical activity for young children, practitioners should remain mindful of the fact that no one area of Learning and Development in the EYFS is more important than another. However, adults working with young children need to critically evaluate their provision, ensuring that enough time is actually provided for Physical Development. The question is: how is this possible?

● *Timetable it.* Ensure that there are designated times during each session when children have access to the outdoor play area, the school hall and/or the local park.

● *Integrate it.* Use cross-curricular links to ensure that Physical Development takes place as an integral feature of provision in the setting. (See Section 8 for a plethora of Ideas.)

● *Teach through it.* Use physical activity as a way of helping children to learn – for example, washing hands, tending to flowers through gardening, and feeling one's own heart beat after running around for a minute.

● *Equal-access it.* Work to provide a balance of indoor and outdoor provision for all children by colour-coding the planning. Is there an equal share of yellow (indoor) and orange (outdoor)?

● *Short-burst it.* Provide quick two-minute bursts of activity sporadically throughout the session to keep children mentally alert.

● *Encourage it outside.* Talk to parents and carers about children engaging in physical activity outside of the setting to support learning and teaching that have taken place inside. Use leaflets, posters, flyers and letters as alternatives.

Setting Up and Clearing Away Resources

Good early years practice is, by its very nature, quite heavily resource-laden, and practitioners need to develop systems and strategies to ensure that standards of health and safety and organization are maintained and developed. Knowing how to achieve this is not the driving force of this Idea; it is more about how we can make this time more physically active.

- *Labels, labels everywhere.* Create handwritten and ICT-produced laminated labels with the children so that it is clear what is stored in each container. Use images, photographs or drawn representations to support children who are not ready to read.

- *Colour-coded class.* Keep sets of mixed resources together by ensuring that they are all the same colour. For example, all the blue items (bats, balls, hoops, ropes (handles), quoits, jumping spots, etc.) are kept in the blue box – and similarly for other colours.

- *Mark out your territory.* Use chalk or masking tape to mark out where you want adults and children to set up and return resources for play activities – for example, trikes in numbered bays. The same system can also be used to organize store cupboards.

- *Boxes doing a wheelie.* Purchase large storage boxes with wheels so that children can help set up and clear away resources by wheeling these out and returning them as and when necessary. Alternatively, mount boxes on go-kart-style bases made in the setting by the children.

- *Cover, cover, gone.* Put plastic sheeting over outdoor resources when not in use to protect them from the sun, the rain and inquisitive little hands.

- *Rota for you and me.* Set up and display fair rotas for practitioners and children to support the setting up and clearing away of resources.

Section 6:
Movements:
Developmental Stages

Crawling the Crawl

It is interesting to note that most formal developmental milestone and learning scales leave crawling off them, because of the wide range of times and methods babies may use to learn to crawl. However, as crawling is a clear indication that babies want to be mobile, let's explore some suggestions, because once they are off, nothing can stop them.

- *Tantalizing toys.* To entice babies to crawl, place toys and other desirable objects, such as shiny paper and yourself, *just* beyond their reach.

- *Confidence, speed and agility.* Build babies' capabilities by distributing pillows, boxes and sofa cushions to create obstacle courses for them to negotiate.

- *Check the childproofing.* Crawling babies can become a little 'mischievous' once on the move, so ensure that the setting is childproof: stair gates are installed, electric sockets are covered, and fragile items and lightweight freestanding objects, including plants, are removed.

- *Big crawling.* Give children a helping hand by modelling how to crawl, supporting them physically by holding them by the elbows.

- *Tummy-tastic.* Children may not want to crawl because they do not like lying on their stomachs or are not given enough opportunities to get used to this. Place firm foam rollers under the child's upper body so that they can face you, allowing you to talk to them, amuse and encourage them. In time this will make tummy-lying a more pleasant experience.

- *Alternatives to crawling.* A bit of bottom shuffling, sliding on their tummies, pulling themselves up, standing up and walking are all possibilities that young children may engage with. As long as they are moving, it does not matter, so do not worry if the children you work with do not crawl.

Walking the Walk

Learning to walk is one of the most important milestones in a child's life. It indicates a huge step towards their independence. Children take their first steps between the ages of 9 months and 17 months, but the exact time is dependent on the support, experiences and encouragement from practitioners and parents and carers, hence this Idea.

● *Coordinated strongman.* Support children in learning to sit, roll over and crawl to build up their muscle strength and coordination. They will then move on to pulling themselves up and standing. After that, it's a matter of confidence and balance.

● *Fortunate furniture.* Help young children to cruise (moving around upright while holding on to furniture) by making different items accessible and safe for them to grasp by adopting childproofing recommendations.

● *'Bend ze knees.'* Babies are likely to find sitting after standing a little tricky. Instead of picking them up and putting them down on the floor, show them how to bend their knees to maintain balance and control over their actions.

● *Encouraging those first steps.* Support children in their attempts to walk by standing or kneeling in front of them and holding out your hands, holding both their hands and walking them towards you, or buying a 'toddle truck' that they can hold on to and push.

● *Say no to carrying.* Children are only going to be able to develop their walking skills if they are given opportunities to practise these, through, for example, visits to the park, and walking around, or to or from, the home or setting. Pick up children only when it is necessary, such as when they are tired, physically hurt or wanting a quick cuddle.

IDEA

53

Running the Run

If there is one movement that epitomizes childhood, it is running. Children love to run, and whilst it is to be expected that they will do so with a certain level of success, it is important for practitioners to consider those children who require a little more encouragement so that they too relish the experience of 'feeling the wind through their hair', while keeping the action interesting and purposeful for those with a zest for running.

- *Take flight.* Encourage children to exaggerate the 'flight' part of their run (where neither foot has contact with the ground) by 'flying' through the air with wide arms and legs.

- *Race against time.* Set up lots of running races of different distances and different pathways. Link these to 'Olympics' role play.

- *Running robots.* Instruct your 'little robots' to run in different directions: forwards, backwards and sideways. Issue your commands in a robotic voice.

- *Closed and open.* Set up areas both inside and outside where children can run freely (open) and where they have to navigate their way around resources, obstacles and other children (closed).

- *Cartoon capers.* Show children examples of Billy Whizz (from the comic *The Beano*), inviting the children to mimic his behaviour – speeding around. Alternatives include Dash from *The Incredibles,* Road Runner and Speedy Gonzales.

- *Whoooosh!* Work with children to consider how their running technique would change if they were running from a giant through a meadow, over a high bridge, under a series of low trees or in between closely stacked boxes.

Jumping the Jump

If you were asked to recall the image that best represents the musical (and film) *Fame*, you would probably describe young people jumping into the air with huge smiles on their faces. Our goal is for the children we work with to have this 'spring in their step' and to relish the opportunity to fly up into the air. So, come on one and all: Jump! Jump! Jump!

- *Blast off*. Use jumping actions to represent rockets shooting into space, fireworks flying into the sky, and streamers from party poppers leaping into the air.

- *Pull up*. Help children to practise the springing action of their legs by encouraging them to pull themselves up into the air via fences, walls, nets, posts, gates and balance bars.

- *Musical madness*. Get children to jump as and where appropriate when listening to 'Reach for the Stars' by S Club 7, 'Jump' by Girls Aloud, 'Jump Around' by House of Pain, and 'Jump' by Kris Kross.

- *Prepositional jumping*. Support different ways of jumping with problem-solving, reasoning and numeracy vocabulary, such as *in* puddles, *on* spots, *over* cones, *into* the wagon, *out of* boxes, *across* the river (blue wiggly fabric on the floor).

- *Warm-up jumping*. Get those star jumps and jumping jacks on the go to get the heart rate up and the legs moving.

- *'Jumping for joy.'* A wonderful topic that could last for a week, during which children could play with pogo sticks, skipping ropes and small trampolines.

- *Animal magic*. Replicate the jumping movements of kangaroos, rabbits, frogs, crickets, grasshoppers, horses, spiders and dolphins (jumping out of the water).

Climbing the Climb

There are many different things that young children like to climb – ladders, trees, poles and furniture – many of which need some adult supervision to ensure their health and safety. One key climbing resource is stairs, which children are infinitely curious about, and which frighten practitioners and parents and carers – 'Are they going to fall?'

● *Going up.* Provide children with opportunities to go up the stairs in different ways: walking up with one foot on each step, two feet meeting on one step before moving up to the next one, or two feet at the same time.

● *Coming down.* Encourage children to hold on to the banister or lean against the wall using their shoulder, using their feet as in 'Going up' but moving down the stairs instead.

● *Various steps.* Try to vary the kind of steps children actually negotiate – stone, carpeted, natural, brick, wooden – so that they provide different challenges and encourage different degrees of care and consideration for individuals.

● *Background support.* When children initially attempt to go up or down stairs, ensure that you are behind them so that you are able to catch them if they fall back on you going up, or in front of them so you can catch them if they fall forwards on to you when coming down.

● *Confidence levels.* Build children's confidence levels by setting challenges – for example, can you make it up four steps all on your own? Build up the number of steps until the child is able to scale the stairs in one continuous sequence of movement.

Balancing the Balance

Young children need plenty of opportunities to develop their sense of balance, which takes many years to refine and control. Practitioners need to ensure that their provision primarily supports children through static and dynamic balances. The first two suggestions are designed to do this.

- *Static balances.* Start with simple balancing by momentarily standing on one foot. Build this up so children are able to stand on alternate feet for three to five seconds. Can they extend this to ten seconds, ensuring that their body remains upright?

- *Dynamic balances.* Help children to build skills of balancing while combining movements by providing benches, ropes, balance beams, bridges, ladders laid flat on the floor, or a collection of tyres for children to explore.

- *Body shape balances.* Support children in emphasizing body shapes when still or moving – for example, wide, narrow, twisted, bent, straight, round, symmetrical or asymmetrical ones. Link these shapes to different types of trees that may be found in a forest.

- *Static and dynamic as one.* Work with children to create small sequences of static and dynamic balances. For example, have them stand on one leg and then walk along a rope before performing an upright balance at the end.

- *Balance tips.* Guide children to perform the best balances by thinking about where their head is and where they are looking. Talk about their breathing and help them to extend their arms where possible to create a strong central line.

- *Testing one's balance.* Offer children opportunities to balance beanbags on different parts of their body, use trampolines, work on spongy mats or sand, play games such as hopscotch, stand on squidgy discs and balance boards, and bounce on space hoppers to challenge their ability to balance.

Kicking the Kick

Football, one of the most popular sports in the United Kingdom, obviously relies largely on players being able to kick the ball. Preparations for adults to be able to do so begin in the EYFS, so let us examine ways in which we can draw children into the wonder of giving footballs a good 'welly'.

- *Distance, not accuracy.* When working with children, initially encourage them to kick just for distance rather than accuracy.

- *Balls for all.* Provide a ball for every child unless you are encouraging them to work in pairs or small groups.

- *Driven by exploration.* Let young children learn by exploring the ball on their own, encouraging them to work on stationary balls prior to a moving ball.

- *Left and right.* Encourage children to kick with both their preferred and their non-preferred foot, talking through the difficulties they may encounter: body position, uncomfortable sensations through the body, lack of control.

- *Pendulum swing.* Help children to build a kick that swings back and kicks 'through' the ball to ensure distance challenges are achieved and exceeded.

- *Skills breakdown.* Help children to kick balls by breaking the skill down into small chunks. For example, focus just on body positioning, movement of legs, use of arms, position of head. Subsequently, build these up by combining aspects together.

- *Where to kick and with what.* Allow children to find out what happens when they kick the ball at the top, in the middle, either side or at the bottom using different parts of their feet such as the toes (a high ball), the inside portion of the foot (a ground ball) and the top portion of their foot (a low ball).

Throwing the Throw

Children have the potential to be much further on in their throwing capabilities in the EYFS but can be hindered by inadequate instructions, opportunities for practice and encouragement from practitioners. This Idea is about addressing these issues, offering ways to ensure that the fundamental movement of throwing is developed when and wherever possible.

- *What to throw*. Vary what children throw by selecting from beanbags, newspaper balls, yarn balls, stocking balls, cotton wool balls and table tennis balls. Exciting alternatives include balls with streamers attached to them, shuttlecocks, Frisbees and silks.

- *Ways to throw*. Encourage children to throw objects in different ways: overarm, underarm and sidearm, using one or both hands. It is important for children to have the opportunity to experience these different movements and then to select the most appropriate one to aid the purpose of their throwing.

- *Distance first, speed second, accuracy third*. Ensure that children are initially encouraged to throw for distance only. Support the children by working with them on the speed at which they are attempting to throw, followed by the accuracy.

- *A ready supply of throwing objects*. Build excitement and opportunities to practise by having to hand baskets of objects for individuals to throw. Invite other children to collect them once they have all been thrown, returning them to the basket in the fastest time possible. Who can collect the most?

- *What to throw to*. Provide children with opportunities to throw towards different things such as to another person, at another person (soft foam balls only), into a bucket, over a rope, under a hoop, through a tube, at a wall, into the air, down to the ground, on to a hopscotch grid and towards a target board on the wall.

Catching the Catch

It is a wondrous moment when the children we work with are able to catch a ball. It signifies a child's ability to track moving objects with their eyes, coordinate their arms and hands, and anticipate and perform actions at the right time. This complex series of capabilities can only be really developed if children are given plenty of opportunities to practise, refine and develop their skills – hence the suggestions below, which support this aim.

- *Various hands*. Support children in catching with two hands, building this up to using one hand – both left and right – until children develop a preference.

- *Size is important*. When helping children to catch balls, think big, allowing them to catch beach balls and balloons. Once they are comfortable catching large balls, provide smaller ones to challenge their capabilities.

- *Lots to catch*. Vary the kind of things children catch, such as wet sponges, giant air-flow balls, foam rugby balls, beanbags, hoops and hats.

- *Alternative catches*. Model different ways of catching objects, such as in a bag, in a net, in a hat, in a bucket, in a T-shirt or in a plastic scoop.

- *Catching off two feet*. Most practitioners encourage children to catch when they are standing on both feet. Add a little challenge by getting them to sit down, kneel, stand on a bench, stand on one leg, lie on their back and even lie on their front.

- *Classic catching*. Many children adopt a 'crocodile snapping' approach to catching whereby their hands come together like a set of crocodile's teeth snapping together. Model how to keep your hands together, pulling your hands towards your chest as your fingers close around the object you are catching; think like a cricketer.

- *On the move*. Catching objects while in a stationary position is common practice in early years settings, so why not get children to catch objects while on the move? They could blow bubbles, or bounce rubber balls set free by the practitioner.

- *Tumbling teddies*. Set up a row of teddy bears on a shelf or a wall. Gently knock them off one by one in a random order. Can the children catch them before they fall in the basket underneath them?

- *Cloud catching*. Stand on a chair and drop white hankies or large cotton balls to represent clouds for the children to catch.

Striking the Strike

Being able to hold an object (e.g. a bat), swing it, and successfully have contact with another object (a ball) that either has been thrown to them or is stationary involves a complex series of capabilities which demonstrate various skills that need to be developed individually and combined with others. The following are ways in which children can gain valuable experiences in hitting, swinging and striking objects (not each other!).

- *Game bats, sticks and clubs.* Have them practise swinging actions with child-friendly plastic cricket bats, tennis rackets, rounders bats, golf clubs, table tennis bats, badminton rackets, baseball bats and hockey sticks.

- *Striking cues.* It may seem unusual, but consider providing children with age-friendly versions of snooker, pool and billiards games to develop gripping and moving actions.

- *Game play.* Playing crazy golf and shuffleboard are just two games that promote striking actions in a child-friendly and easily accessible way.

- *Big to small.* Provide larger objects such as beach balls to strike initially, using plastic tennis rackets to build children's self-esteem.

- *Stationary and moving.* Ensure a balance of moving targets (balls being thrown to them) and stationary targets (golf balls on tees, baseballs on tubing) in your provision.

- *Long and short.* Audit your provision of equipment for children to use to strike with. Are there more short-handed or more long-handed pieces available for the children to use?

- *Rule of thumb.* There is really only one rule in striking: keep your eye on the ball. It couldn't be simpler.

Section 7:
Learning and Teaching in Physical Development

Various Vocabularies

An essential aspect of any physical activity is the promotion and use of language to develop knowledge, skills and action. Practitioners should ensure that when they are planning activities, whether child-initiated or adult-led, they consider the most appropriate vocabulary to support, extend and enrich provision. Consider using the following in your future planning and practice:

- *The vocabulary of movement.* Crash, jump, hop, run, skip, walk, run
- *The vocabulary of power.* Pound, pelt, push, shove, force, plunge, punch, thrust, strong, strength
- *The vocabulary of quickness.* Fast, zoom, whizz, whoosh, zing, accelerate, rapid, express, quick, speedy, flee
- *The vocabulary of stillness.* Settle, still, rest, motionless, frozen, numb, calm
- *The vocabulary of shaking.* Sizzle, fizz, wave, quiver, tremble, shrug, sway, bubbling
- *The vocabulary of opening and closing.* Enclose, fold, wrap, unfold, spread, surround, open, close
- *The vocabulary of lightness.* Feathery, flutter, gentle, softly, drift, fly, sail, fluffy, light
- *The vocabulary of slowness.* Smooth, creep, crawl, calm, wispy, sweep, trundle, swagger, lull
- *The vocabulary of unease.* Sway, bob, drift, wobble, flutter, hover, waddle, wilt
- *The vocabulary of sound.* Bang, boom, stomp, crash, wallop, tap, knock, pop, burst, rap, explode, clatter, crackle, clash, zing, whizz, whoosh
- *The vocabulary of sharpness.* Chop, slice, sudden, flinch, duck, grab, catch, bash, lash.

Practitioners are encouraged to add to these lists as and when appropriate, modelling them in their spoken instructions and discussions. Laminated word cards, either suspended on mobiles, fastened to walls or resources, or written in chalk on the outdoor play area floor, are useful ways of reminding all practitioners of vocabulary in need of 'promotion'.

Time to Cool Down

Cooling down is an important part of any physical activity work for children, just as warming up is (see Idea 44). Both are more likely to be an integral part of indoor hall work as opposed to practice linked to the outdoor play area. This Idea is all about getting practitioners to ensure that at least one minute is dedicated to ensuring that children's bodies are suitably 'calmed down' following outdoor exertions.

- *Body shapes.* Ask the children to stand in a space and create a shape with their bodies – square, triangle, tall shape, wiggly – using very slow and careful movements.

- *Stretch me.* Gently stretch the arms, legs, hands, neck, feet and the waist using the beat of gentle background music to ensure consistent time limits to each stretch.

- *Point and rub.* Ask children to point to different parts of their body, extending the names of these for the more able – for example, thorax, quads, biceps, temple. Once a body part has been located, ask children to rub that part (where appropriate), massaging it with smooth movements.

- *Better breathing.* Help children to regulate their breathing with slow, deep lungfuls of air, feeling their chest inflate and deflate with their hands as they inhale and exhale.

- *Lie and lift.* Ask children to lie on their backs with their eyes closed. Instruct them to lift up certain body parts off the floor, extending this for the more able by asking for left or right body parts. Have them shake these body parts gently and then return them to the floor.

- *Time slows down.* Play 'Follow My Leader' (with you as the leader) but gradually slow down your movements until you completely stop. An alternative is 'Draining batteries', where you all pretend to put new batteries in your bodies, which slowly run down.

IDEA

63

Allowing Skills to Permeate through the Planning

When practitioners sit to plan individually or as part of a group, it is important that they ensure a balance of skills through the activities they set up for the day, or week. Awareness of the different physical skills will allow practitioners to be in a stronger position to provide breadth, scope and variety to their provision.

- *Gross and fine.* Plan for children to pretend to be an athlete who runs, jumps and throws (gross) while working in role as an artist, modelling with clay and plasticine (fine).

- *Open and closed.* Plan activities where children are able to practise repeatedly kicking a ball from a fixed point (closed) but they also have opportunities to dribble the ball around cones and other obstacles (open).

- *Self-paced and externally paced.* Plan games that allow children to roll and chase hoops around the play area at a selected speed (self-paced) while setting up challenges to chase and catch as many hoops as they can, the hoops being released at different speeds by a practitioner (externally paced).

- *Discrete, serial or continuous.* Use resources that encourage children to develop discrete skills: short movements with a clear start and finish, for example bats to hit a ball, scoops to catch a beanbag. By contrast, continuous skills require children to make repeated movements, such as walking with imaginary clowns' shoes on or running with wellington boots on. Serial skills are discrete in nature yet are performed together in a sequence. For example, the children could follow a dance routine (e.g. the Locomotion, the Macarena, the Cha-Cha Slide or Saturday Night), or move between a series of benches and mats using repeated twirling and hopping actions.

Providing Child-Initiated Learning Opportunities

Child-initiated learning is an essential part of quality practice in EYFS; if children are to understand what is being taught (through adult-led activities), they need to be provided with time and space to use and apply their growing knowledge and skills in a range of purposeful contexts. So, how do we ensure this for children in terms of their physical development?

● *Luscious lavatories.* For young children to understand basic bodily functions and manage their personal hygiene, ensure there is adequate soap, towels, tissues, water and small steps available.

● *Specially selected literature.* Provide illustrated cookery books in the 'kitchen' and food magazines in the 'living room' role-play areas to promote the importance of food and drink in their lives.

● *Floor markings.* Chalk out hopscotch and snakes and ladders grids along with 'tracks' in the form of footprints, wiggly lines or spots for children to use and follow to develop coordination and control over large movements.

● *Obstacle courses.* Set up courses with 'A' frames, plastic crates, steps, spots, planks, tunnels and ladders to develop children's abilities to navigate and explore space, including around, through, over, under, in between, and so on.

● *Lovely links.* Set up activities that combine physical development with other areas or aspects of Learning and Development. For example, the children could use squeezy or pump bottles and pipettes with paints for outdoor spray painting (CD), or walk or crawl over natural and non-natural materials (KUW).

● *Mark-making for the masses.* Provide a range of writing implements such as crayons, Hand Huggers, colouring pencils, chunky chalks, HB pencils, felt-tip and dry-wipe pens to support children at different stages in their manipulative control and dexterity.

Planning for Adult-Led Learning Activities

Effective practice in the early years recommends that practitioners not only provide opportunities for child-initiated learning but also offer planned adult-led activities and experiences. Below are a selection of quality adult-led activities that span all aspects of physical development.

- *Visits*. Arrange visits from nurses, dentists, health visitors or a parent with a baby to develop health and bodily awareness and stimulate potential role-play activities. Visits to cafés, shops and markets are recommended to support learning about healthy foods and drinks.

- *Wonderful woodwork*. Using close supervision, develop children's confidence and control over hammers, saws, drills, clamps and pliers. Make artefacts linked to current topics, for example a bird box for autumn (KUW link), a spice rack for creative cooking (CD link) or bookstands for Parkview Publishers (CLL link).

- *Jumping jacks*. Build up patterns of jumps with the children to help them develop, coordinate and control movements. For example, two star jumps on the spot could be followed by three jumps to the left, four jumps forwards and one *Fame*-style jump at the end.

- *Cookery class*. It may be messy, but cooking with young children is invaluable in helping them to use tools to perform certain actions, such as stirring, rolling, kneading and cutting.

- *Throw yourself into it*. Practically model different throwing skills for children to support, extend and challenge their capabilities. Throw beanbags in the air, forwards, sideways, at a target, into a container, over a held rope, backwards, across the body and towards the ground.

IDEA 66

Quality Teaching Strategies

Irrespective of whether the children you work with are 5 months or 5 years old, it is important to have a bank of teaching strategies to hand so that you can effectively move their knowledge, skills and understanding forwards when and where appropriate. Here are some of the best suggestions available. Use this as a checklist to assess your own strengths and areas for consideration:

- *Work it.* Be a role model for children. Look the part (that is, dress appropriately), ooze enthusiasm and be prepared to show children what you mean.

- *Crystal clear.* Give articulate and comprehensive instructions and explanations so that children are clear about what they are to do and how they are to do it.

- *Eyes and ears of a hawk.* Keep your eyes and ears open when you are observing children, asking other adults to make written notes as you verbalize your thoughts and observations.

- *Leave 'em to it.* Provide children with ample time to explore, experiment and practise skills they have acquired without adults hovering or commenting on their actions or efforts.

- *Challenges for children.* Set children 'Can you . . .?', 'I bet you can't . . .', 'Are you able to . . .?' and 'Who's better at . . .?' tasks to promote healthy competition and activity.

- *Ofsted me!* Show children a certain movement or skill and ask them to talk with you about what was good about it and what could be improved. With younger children, you may have to offer them suggestions to select from.

- *Learner-led.* Provide children with a range of resources and ask them to develop a skill or a sequence of their choice. Practitioners may need to direct younger children – *Practitioner-led.*

Encouraging Learning to Take Place

No one tells a baby to reach out and take hold of a toy or a teething ring, so how is it that young children learn to develop physically? When planning for Physical Development, practitioners need to consider exactly how they will encourage the children they work with to learn, and this can usually be achieved by recognizing the different modes of learning:

● *Make it accidental*. Through repetition and enjoyment, babies are likely to learn that movement with resources such as mobiles and rattles result in certain effects, say movement and noise.

● *Causal calamity*. Cause and effect, which underpins this type of learning, is usually the result of children's trial and error. Allow children to kick different-sized balls to establish which one travels the furthest.

● *Excellent experimentation*. Give children the opportunity to explore, free from time and space constraints. This kind of play – child-initiated – is complemented by practitioner support – adult-led.

● *Imitate me*. Children learn by copying, so encourage them to observe practitioners and other children and to mimic their movements.

● *Do us a demo*. Be a role model and show children what you mean so that they can aspire to be you or other children by trying to become the 'expert'.

● *Follow my instructions*. Give children short, easy-to-follow sequential instructions that will help them to achieve a certain action, movement or skill.

Music and Sound to Support Learning and Teaching

Think of dance and you automatically think of music; the two are intrinsically linked. Every setting will have a collection of CDs and tapes to stimulate children's dance work but few offer a true breadth of musical types to develop and extend movement. Consider adding some of the following types of music to enrich your collections:

- hip-hop (take care with the lyrics)
- classical
- pop
- R&B (take care with the lyrics)
- garage (take care with the lyrics)
- 1960s rock and roll
- jazz
- soul
- elevator music
- boy and girl bands
- electro-funk
- Motown
- roaring twenties
- religious
- contemporary
- 1950s big band
- opera
- folk music
- Christmas
- rap
- love songs – 'the smoothies'
- heavy metal (take care with the lyrics)
- punk (take care with the lyrics)

- bhangra
- rock
- disco
- urban (take care with the lyrics)
- blues
- swing
- trance
- salsa
- pan pipes
- easy listening
- acid jazz
- dance
- film
- electronic
- country and western
- flamenco
- musicals
- techno
- brass band
- morris dancing
- Latin American – tango

Recommendations from the Shop Floor

While this book is not designed to be just another collection of 'tips for practitioners', it will be useful to dedicate at least one Idea to a collection of tips, strategies and supporting ideas suggested by real practitioners during the writing of this book. Consider the potential impact of these on raising standards in Physical Development in your own setting.

- *Get them outside.* The outdoors is as important as the indoors; ensure you provide children with plenty of opportunities to get outside. Take advantage of space and resources available at local sports centres, soft play centres and parks. Ignore the weather (whenever possible).

- *Seeing is believing.* Plan opportunities for practitioners to model movements, actions and skills that children can copy, develop and extend themselves. Use DVDs, video and the internet to show footage of movement in action.

- *Keep it varied.* Maintain children's attention and energy levels by providing them with a range of different resources and experiences so that they are able to build on their previous successes. Avoid putting out the same stuff every day.

- *Strong links.* See Physical Development as both a separate and an integral part of the curriculum, using links with other areas, and aspects of learning, to strengthen learning and experiences. Embrace creativity.

- *Track those milestones.* Children have milestones to achieve in terms of their physical development. Work to use these as a way of driving standards and experiences (see http://loyolauniversity.adam.com/content. aspx?productId=101&pid=1&gid=002002).

- *Give them time to explore.* Step back and give children time and space to explore, experiment, and refine and develop their knowledge, skills and understanding. You can learn a great deal about a child by simply observing them.

Section 8:
Links with Other Areas and Aspects of Learning and Development

Making Links with PSED 1

Dispositions and Attitudes, Self-Confidence and Self-Esteem, Making Relationships

PSED is an important area of Learning and Development, as those children without a positive sense of themselves and others, respect for others, social skills and a positive disposition to learn will find life very difficult. Links with Physical Development will help to put these essential aspects of PSED into a real and valuable context, as shown by the following suggestions:

- *Leave me be and be with me.* Plan times to stand back and simply let babies and young children explore and experiment with aspects of physical development on their own. Plan times to interact with them, offering encouragement and both individual and group challenges.

- *Sky high.* Allow children to make decisions as to how they will use different resources. For example, when using beanbags, children may want to throw or catch them, balance them on their heads and/or run around with them. Praise and record achievements, boosting the children's self-esteem.

- *It's your choice.* Provide children with a plethora of culturally diverse drinks and snacks to reveal preferences, while offering opportunities to try something new and exciting such as kiwi, mango, cherries or prunes.

- *No 'I' in 'Team'!* Set up game-play opportunities that encourage children to collaborate together, share and take turns. Organize and support children so that they can lead game play, reinforcing rules and agreed forms of behaviour.

- *Come join in.* Frequently ask children to look around and invite others to join in with activities led by either themselves or practitioners. Use a chant to promote this, such as 'Can you spy with your little eye someone who wants to join in?'

- *Follow my lead.* Use confident children to model ways of jumping off an object, as an example for others to replicate and experiment with. Offer alternatives where appropriate, for example legs together, legs crossed, hands behind back, arms and legs out wide like a star.

Making Links with PSED 2

Behaviour and Self-Control, Self-Care, Sense of Community

Many creative links can be made with all aspects of PSED, particularly with those associated with the three strands identified above. Practitioners are strongly advised to be mindful of these when planning for physical activity in the long, medium and short term.

- *'Once, twice, three times a go.'* Set up (as an example) a group of different obstacle courses to reduce conflict, and ensure that children get a good number of opportunities to tackle them.

- *Reasonable rules*. Work with the children to formulate a small number of agreed rules for physical activity. Display these in creative ways such as laminated on resources, written in chalk on the outdoor play area floor, or on mobiles. Create and follow rules for simple games as well.

- *Ahhh – refreshing!* Have plastic cups and jugs of water readily available, both inside and outside, to develop children's independence and social skills.

- *Fabulous food*. Invite children to share and try foods from different cultures, talking about healthy options. Make these available on the 'refreshments' table alongside the water (see *Ahhh – refreshing!* above).

- *Understanding disability*. Help children to appreciate how those with diverse physical characteristics can engage in physical activity, for example by hurling beanbags while sitting on chairs, kicking balls using just one leg, throwing Velcro darts while wearing a blindfold.

- *Only donkeys kick*. Help children to understand how their actions have consequences by using animal movement analogies – for example, 'Only bears bite!' 'Only parrots pinch!' 'Only joeys jump the queue!'

Making Links with CLL 1

Language for Communication, Language for Thinking

The value of language, particularly spoken language, in children's lives cannot be overestimated and should be promoted, developed and extended wherever and whenever possible. Physical Development offers plenty of opportunities for practitioners and children to communicate with each other, so let's use some written language to explore a few of these.

- *Meaningful sounds.* Work to encourage, interpret and respond to noises children make associated with physical activity, such as panting, laughter, screaming, talking and short breathing.

- *Mixed messages.* Build children's vocabulary by using key words and phrases in simple and more complex sentences – for example, '*Kick* the ball', or 'Would you *roll* the tyre slowly over to James, please?'

- *Chants galore.* Develop children's sense of rhythm, intonation and phrasing, along with their self-motivation to get involved with physical activity, by making up and teaching chants to be recited during little running races, sports days and tidy up time.

- *Instruct me, please.* Allow children to instruct others when learning and playing new games, combining words and actions to demonstrate, model and challenge others.

- *Talking food.* Talk through physical processes when making lunch with the children, inviting them to discuss what needs to come next, thus promoting sequencing and thinking skills.

- *Actions speak louder than words.* Encourage individuals to make different movements, asking others to guess what 'doing word' individuals were thinking of. Examples include Dig! Ski! Rock! Slide! Dance!

- *Sequencing movements.* Model 'thinking alouds' by creating and putting together movements in response to music or other stimuli.

Making Links with CLL 2

Linking Sounds and Letters, Reading, Writing and Handwriting

Practitioners are becoming increasingly creative in terms of finding ways to make CLL more 'physical' so that children do not become 'cooked' by lots of static and repetitive learning and teaching experiences. Here are some further suggestions to make 'em move more:

- *Sound effects.* Collect resources that make sounds and help to develop children's gross and fine motor skills, for example tap shoes that need to be danced in, bubble wrap that needs to be squeezed.

- *Reading through movement.* Read stories to children which use a lot a movement as part of the tale. Examples include 'The Three Billy Goats Gruff' or 'The Three Little Pigs'. Encourage children to 'work in role', bringing characters to life with their facial expressions and actions.

- *Feed the gross into the fine.* Throw balls, swirl ribbons and rake sand to develop handwriting skills.

- *Movement ABC.* Use systematic phonic schemes that promote physical movement to support and strengthen learning, such as Jolly Phonics (see www.jollylearning.co.uk).

- *Fine motor flaps.* Provide children with books that have various flaps, tabs and pockets, thus encouraging fine motor control and coordination.

- *High-frequency movements.* Develop children's recognition and understanding of words they see regularly by using movements to put them in context, such as 'open' by opening doors, and 'stop' by running and stopping at the 'Stop' road sign.

- *Marvellous mark making.* Develop movement skills by providing a wealth of different writing implements including thick crayons, paintbrushes, chalk, fountain pens and dry-wipe marker pens.

IDEA 74

Making Links with PSRN 1

Numbers as Labels and for Counting

Many educationalists advocate the potential for strengthening children's learning and development in PSRN by making links with Physical Development. As this entire book is about Physical Development, let's look at ways that link with PSRN and can strengthen learning and development in PD through number:

- *Number songs and movements*. Teach and sing songs that encourage children to perform a certain number of actions, such as 'One potato, two potato . . .', '1, 2, 3, 4, 5, Once I caught a fish alive . . .'

- *Matching digits*. Number up bikes and trikes with large digit cards, providing sand timers with matching numbers to give all children a go.

- *Die actions*. Allow children to throw a large die, performing that number of actions – gross and/or fine motor – in response to child and practitioner suggestions.

- *Movement challenges*. Challenge children to perform as many jumps, stamps or bounces as possible in a minute, counting how many they do. Record these with marks or numbers and see if the children can beat their personal best.

- *Fine motor fitness*. Encourage children to count the number of buttons they have to fasten on their coats, or studs on their jackets, before they go outside.

- *Food numbers*. Encourage children to count the number of pieces of fruit given and consumed by others in the setting.

- *Number rules*. Work with the children to create number rules such as 'Only one child on the slide at any one time' and 'Just four children in the sand pit, please!'

IDEA

75

Making Links with PSRN 2

Calculating and Shape, Space and Measures

Practitioners are encouraged to 'recognise the mathematical potential of the outdoor environment' (DfES, 2007: 61) by paying particular attention to learning and development associated with calculating, shape, distance and measures. There are plenty of ways to make this 'potential' a reality:

- *Tidy up time.* Use this time to sort balls, bats, buckets and spades into appropriate boxes, using pictures and images to support children.

- *Random races.* Use races (e.g. running, bike, walking and sack) to put ordinal numbers – 1st, 2nd – into a real context. Count how many children start and finish the races to emphasize cardinal numbers – 1, 2 and 3.

- *More or less.* Invite children to observe physical activity in different parts of the outdoor play area, comparing numbers of children on the bikes and on the climbing frame.

- *TV boxes.* Use large empty TV boxes and 'presenters' to put prepositional language into a real and exciting context, such as in, underneath, and next to.

- *Floor mosaics.* Encourage children to create large floor mosaics using two-dimensional shapes. Photograph images of compositions for assessment purposes.

- *Against my string.* Give each child a different length of string, asking them to run, or skip, or hop, or jump over to items outdoors to find out whether they are shorter, longer or about the same length as their piece of string.

- *Squeezy balls.* Teach children about how objects can change shape by providing stress balls, foam blocks and rubber items which can be squashed and stretched.

- *Fine motor number lines.* Provide children with chalk or brushes and pots of water to create number lines to find one more or one less when, for example, children leave or come to the sand pit.

Making Links with KUW 1 – Designing and Making

Many practitioners are aware of the valuable links Designing and Making has in supporting children's development in the Using Equipment and Materials strand of Physical Development. What they may be less aware of are other ways in which this strand develops knowledge, skills and understanding across the full area of Learning and Development.

- *Sensory stimulation.* Rattles, mobiles and teething rings all provide opportunities for babies to experience textures and materials through their mouths. Older children can experience these through movements with their hands.

- *Building towers.* Help children to develop their grasping, gripping, placing and pushing skills by asking them to create towers using wooden blocks, Lego bricks and foam building blocks.

- *Pushing and pulling.* Use body strength and energy levels to fly kites, pull wheelbarrows, push prams, pull cords to activate bells, and push tyres.

- *Super sticks.* Experiment with sticks and balls of salt dough, seeing how physical force can make holes, create patterns, slice it into pieces, shape it to create a 'toffee apple' and create a model helter-skelter.

- *Arm muscles a-bulging.* Provide opportunities for children to operate staplers, rolling pins, hacksaws and hammers. Use these to create lunchboxes, shelves for outdoor shoes, healthy cakes and booklets about healthy living.

Making Links with KUW 2 – Time and Place

There are a number of exciting ways in which Physical Development can support, enrich and extend Time and Place learning, both inside and outside the range of different settings in which children learn. Do remember that the reverse is also beneficial (Time and Place supporting, enriching and extending Physical Development), as the following suggestions prove:

- *'Reminder' movements.* Encourage children to use both words and physical actions to help relive significant events that happened in their lives, say when they grazed their knee or chased a paper bag.

- *Fine motor pictures.* Allow children to use different threading materials, hammer- and pin-shape sets and/or collage materials to build images of people, events and objects from when they were younger.

- *Visits galore.* Take children on educational visits by walking them to the shops or the local park, using the different play equipment so that they can observe the effects of activities on their bodies. Use this as an opportunity for children to undo, or do up, fastenings on their coats.

- *Old artefacts into new contexts.* Set up opportunities for children to physically use objects from yesteryear in present-day contexts. For example, they could use old watering cans to carry water and sprinkle it on plants.

- *Movements gone by.* Ask the children to show you ways in which they used to move as a baby and ways they can move now, comparing and talking about how they are different.

- *Exciting environments.* Suggest that children explore their outdoor play area by moving towards different features in different ways: 'Can you hop to the tree?' 'How about sidestepping over to the shed?'

Making Links with KUW 3 – Exploration and Investigation, Communities

The links between Physical Development and Knowledge and Understanding of the World are plentiful, particularly as PD is an integral part of the specific stands of KUW identified in the title of this Idea. Practitioners should use the suggestions below as simply a starting point, adapting these to suit their own setting and the needs of their children.

● *Babies a-movin'.* Young children will use movement as a way of exploring their environment. Set up resources (such as magnifying glasses) around the child in order to promote active exploration and investigation.

● *Movements during special occasions.* Talk about the different ways people move when at weddings, funerals, birthday parties, etc., showing pictures or bringing in visitors to model movements and actions.

● *Movement investigations.* Encourage children to jump in puddles, throw beanbags, squash dough, fly kites and operate equipment, not only to establish cause and effect, but also to begin to gain an appreciation of why these things happen.

● *Feelings and movements.* Allow children to show how they are feeling through physical movements. For example, jumping up and down = frustrated; skipping = happy; bowed head = sad.

● *Questions, questions, questions.* Set up activities that promote questions, for example 'Why do you think a football travels further when kicked than a table tennis ball?', 'Why does sugar disappear when you stir it in water?', 'How come stones sink in water and feathers don't?'

● *Music and movement.* Provide a range of music from different cultures, allowing children to interpret the sounds with gross and fine motor movements.

Making Links with CD 1

Being Creative, Responding to Experiences, Expressing and Communicating Ideas, Developing Imagination and Imaginative Play

There are obvious links between Physical Development and Creating Music and Dance, so instead we will look at ways in which practitioners can nurture and promote physical activity in the remaining aspects of Creative Development.

- *Emotive movement.* Encourage babies and children to move in response to their emotions – for example, kicking actions for anger, shrugging shoulders for laugher, jumping for fear or happiness.

- *Finger and thumb theatre.* Provide children with finger puppets and other small toys, which can be used to create a small puppet theatre, thereby developing fine motor control and dexterity.

- *Physical role play.* Support children in using physical actions to represent characters they take on in role-play situations, for example small, purposeful movements when cooking in the kitchen, large movements when chasing the villagers as the scary giant.

- *Moving stories.* Read and respond practically to stories that encourage children to move in different ways. Suitable examples include *The Very Hungry Caterpillar*, *Room on the Broom* and *We're Going on a Bear Hunt*.

- *Box of junk.* Have to hand a collection of resources for children to access as and when they want either to physically make objects, such as crowns, cloaks or magic wands, or to use objects as representation items, such as tubing as a telephone, or a box as a superhero's vehicle . . . *whoosh!*

- *Freeze like a . . .* Develop children's ability to be still by asking them to stand still like, for example, a superhero, a princess, a penguin and a pop star.

IDEA

80

Making Links with CD 2

Exploring Media and Materials, Creating Music and Dance

The nature of creativity passionately advocates children's movement, and so the links between all aspects of CD and PD are plentiful. While many recognize the potential of dance for developing aspects of PD in children, let's look more at how art and music support PD in the 'adults of the future'.

- *Plastic sheeting.* Allow young children to play on large sheets of plastic, making gross and fine motor movements through glitter, rice, sequins, paint and paper.

- *Finger fun.* Provide children with dough, clay and plasticine so that they can use their fingers to create different textures in the material.

- *Huge art.* Plan activities that encourage children to work on sculptures, constructions and paintings on a large scale, providing them with opportunities to develop skills in movement, spatial awareness and the use of equipment.

- *Construction creativity.* Allow children time to build structures that *combine* construction kits, providing appropriate levels of physical challenge in linking pieces and objects together.

- *Songs and actions.* Build up a bank of songs that encourage children to perform movements in both sitting and standing positions.

- *Percussion perfection.* Provide instruments that require children to use their fine motor skills to play them – for example, plucking guitar strings.

- *Musical movement.* Teach children to move in different ways in response to different instruments, for example that they should jump when the tambourine sounds, and crawl when the bells are rung.

- *Lullaby.* Play calming music when children are resting or sleeping, either commercially bought or composed and recorded by the children themselves.

Section 9:
Considerations for
Physical Development

Considering Gender

Many parents and practitioners hold the stereotypical view that boys need more opportunities for energetic physical activity than girls, not just because they have higher levels of testosterone but because boys are kinaesthetic learners and so need to be 'up and doing and moving'. While there is some truth in this, it is important that gender issues are considered when planning for and delivering physical activity opportunities for children to experience.

- *Getting the resources right.* Provide a range of different bikes and trikes, for example, which will appeal to both sexes. Think about the colour, the use of accessories such as baskets and radios, and the designs on safety helmets.

- *Equal access.* Plan for sufficient materials, tools and equipment to be used by both the boys and girls so that each gender group can access learning opportunities otherwise dominated by the other. Examples include items used in construction, books for reading, bats and balls, and baby play.

- *Challenge stereotypical movement.* Encourage boys to 'move' with streamers and ribbons and push the prams around, while getting the girls to use the computers and chase a rugby ball. Show photo images of girls and boys engaging in this new kind of non-stereotypical activity.

- *Boy and girl leaders.* Invite different children to play new games with you, leading others by teaching them how to play the game they have just learned. Mix up groups so that boys and girls can play both with and against each other in varied teams.

- *Varied constructions.* Invite children to build models that appeal to both sexes, such as bedrooms, superhero lairs, stables and garages.

Considering English as an Additional Language

With the Every Child Matters agenda (DfES, 2004) driving inclusive practice for all children, it is essential that practitioners work to ensure that learners' needs are being met through a range of differentiated tasks and materials. Knowing exactly how to do this can be a stumbling block for some practitioners, so the suggestions below are designed to support practitioners and children in a variety of ways:

- *Making it visual.* Ensure that any of the following are available for children to interpret: posters, drawings, sketches, photographs and dual-language vocabulary cards with supporting images, diagrams, storybooks, music and songs.

- *Delightful demonstration.* Young children can gain a great deal from simply watching the performances and actions of others. Give them time to stand, sit and observe you and the children you work with before they engage in purposeful physical activity.

- *Bilingual brilliance.* Utilize the skills of practitioners who can speak two or more languages to support different children with verbal instructions and encouragement. Alternatively, speak to parents and carers, asking them to write down key words in home languages (practitioners should record the phonetic pronunciation as well) so these can be used in play-based learning.

- *Repetition, repetition, repetition.* Emphasize and repeat key words with children to build comprehension and speech – for example (showing a ball) 'Ball! This is a ball! Good – a ball!'

- *Express yourself.* Use exaggerated body language and gestures to communicate your thoughts, ideas and feelings about their physical activity.

Considering Special Educational Needs

The notion of inclusion in all settings is extremely important, especially as it helps to drive commitments to the EYFS. Rather than trying to address all the special educational needs (SEN) that practitioners may encounter in their work, the following suggestions are designed to be used across the SEN spectrum:

- *Keep it open.* Plan activities for children to engage with, leaving them relatively open so that children can access and complete them to their own level of ability. For example, you could ask children to navigate their way through an obstacle course with numerous starting and finishing points.

- *Individualize it, please.* Set up activities that have specific aspects, such as rules and resources, adapted and modified for individual children.

- *Perfectly parallel.* Allow children to engage with two parallel activities that are either next to each other or a distance apart, yet still allow all children to access the activity and the learning. One of these activities is altered to make it suitable for specific children or groups of children.

- *Sports centre support.* Work with local providers to access equipment and resources to support children with particular SEN that the centre can cater for.

- *Support me, please.* Collaborate with practitioners in the setting to ensure that appropriate adult support is given to children who require it in physical activities provided.

Considering Behaviour

Ensuring good behaviour in children during physical activity is paramount so that they do not harm themselves or others. While Idea 71 supports practice partly linked to the Behaviour and Self-Control strand of PSED, this series of suggestions looks more at exploring the practicalities of managing children's behaviour.

- *Referee cards.* Have a small red and a small green card to hand to indicate visually how well children are behaving. Alternatively, use a small, handheld GO, STOP road sign.

- *Read the signs.* If children are becoming restless and irritable, simply take them outside and let them out have a run around. Even if it is raining, get the children to put their coats and wellies on and have a splash in the puddles. Have them see whether they can dodge the rain droplets!

- *Time, please, gentlechildren!* Ensure that there are large sand and electronic timers available so that children get an equal amount of time on the bikes and trikes.

- *Taming wild beasts.* Avoid deducting children's physical activity time for misbehaving. Rather, ask them to take a slow walk or run or march around the edge of the play area as a physical form of 'time out', giving them chance to think about what they have done.

- *'Boys and girls come out to play . . . '* Some children do not want to run around outside, preferring to sit, chat and watch others playing. Provide quiet areas with seating for these children.

- *'Huwhih huwhoo.'* Take a whistle outside with you but use it only for emergencies. Gain children's attention with a tambourine or a football rattle.

IDEA

85

Considering Getting Undressed and Dressed

Recent research indicates that children, particularly in F1 and F2 settings, can be physically active for less than 15 minutes of a 40-minute hall session, largely because of the amount of time it takes for them to change. How, therefore, do we speed up the changing process to maximize the time children have to engage with focused Physical Development work? Well . . .

● *Parental persuasion.* Encourage parents and carers to work at home with their child, teaching them how to undress and dress themselves in the morning and at night.

● *Challenge and reward me.* Offer challenges and incentives to get the children changed quickly. For example, you could give stickers and stamps to the quickest changers.

● *Against the clock.* Time the children to see how quickly the class as a whole can change into their PE kits. Record this time on a large grid, seeing whether the children can work together to beat the time on consecutive occasions.

● *Elastic fantastic.* Ensure, if you can, that children's shorts and pumps are elasticated to reduce the time needed to deal with laces, straps and strings.

● *Fine motor challenges.* Prepare tasks to promote fine motor control once children have changed. Suitable examples include cutting along different lines with scissors, or threading beads on to a string.

● *Hall time.* If your hall time is the first session of the morning, ask children to come to the setting in their PE kits, changing into their uniform after hall time.

Considering Talented Children

It is likely that you will encounter children in your setting who you may consider to be talented – those with high potential in physical education. They may be only 3 years old, for example, but are able to kick a football with precision, perform complex sequences of gymnastic movements, or serve a tennis ball with force. Whatever their talent, we need to consider how we can effectively meet their needs in our provision.

● *Pulling together.* Work in partnership with local sports centres, local organizations and local national governing bodies to support children, parents and practitioners in developing enhanced policy and practice.

● *Action-plan it.* Work with SEN coordinators and practitioners in classes or settings with older children to formulate individual education plans.

● *PE(n) pals.* Organize chances for children with physical talents to visit and work with other talented children in their setting or other settings.

● *Me? A role model?!* Encourage talented children to show their talents to others so that their knowledge, skills and understanding can be used as an example for others to observe, admire and learn from.

● *Differentiate me.* Ensure that physical activities offer talented children suitable challenges that not only stretch their capabilities but supplement and enrich their experiences outside of the setting.

● *After-school clubs.* Work to ensure that clubs in the setting cater for abilities through local authority support, reading academic literature, speaking to consultants, and accessing websites and e-journals.

● *Listen and learn.* Talk to the children themselves about what they would like to do, asking *them* for guidance, ideas and activities.

Considering Differentiation

For children to engage in physical activity effectively, practitioners need to ensure that opportunities for learning are suitably differentiated so that every child is able to access activities and achieve at their own personal level. There are many ways in which this can be achieved:

- *STEPS it.* Differentiate provision by varying the different SPACES the children are allowed to work in, the different amounts of TIME they are given to engage with and develop activities, the different kinds of EQUIPMENT the children are encouraged to use, the different PEOPLE the children work with, and the differing levels of SUPPORT given by practitioners to individuals so that they are able to achieve their potential.

- *CPP it.* Adopt the CPP approach to differentiation: CONTENT, PROCESS and PRODUCT. For example, your focus could be on throwing (content) but you may have some children throwing beanbags, others with table tennis balls and others with beach balls. Some children may be throwing from a standing position, others may be sitting and some may be running (process). The product could be some children hitting the ball towards a wall, others getting their ball into a basket with others throwing it as far as they can.

- *Open-end it.* DfES (now the DCFS) publications advocate this approach, setting open-ended tasks that allow children to respond at different levels. In practice, these tasks might include building the strongest tower using 15 bricks, running through an obstacle course in the fastest time and linking three appropriate movements together in response to a short piece of music.

- *Teach it.* Good differentiation requires practitioners to consider the best way they can teach the children they work with. See Idea 66 for different teaching strategies to suit different children.

IDEA 88

Considering Health and Safety

No book about Physical Development would be complete without giving some consideration to the importance of health and safety. Many settings ensure quality provision and practice by making this a top priority, but not to such an extent that it stifles the adventurous spirit of children. But how can this approach be applied to all settings?

- *Managing risk.* All PD activities carry some degree of risk, so work with children to develop their own ability to manage this and take appropriate safety measures. For example, make sure they know they must wear a helmet when on the bikes, and keep their eyes open when running.

- *Signal issues.* Use a sound or a sign to indicate when you want children to stop playing – for example, 'When the tambourine is shaken, please stand still and put both hands in the air.' Use a whistle only when an emergency occurs.

- *Self-checking.* Teach children to quickly check the area they are playing in and the equipment they will be using *before* they use it.

- *Gently up and down.* Good practice advocates children doing a gentle warm-up on the carpet area before they access the outdoor play area. When they come back inside, do a gentle cool-down, talking about the importance of these activities. See Ideas 44 and 62 for further suggestions.

- *Snap-shot judgements.* Select one child and, as a group, assess whether they are 'ready' to engage in physical activity, focusing on footwear, hair, jewellery and clothing. Take into consideration cultural differences but make children (and parents and carers) aware of the dangers of inappropriate choices.

IDEA 89

Considering Assessment

'Look, listen and note', one of the four columns that break up each Learning and Development area in the Practice Guidance for the Early Years Foundation Stage (DfES, 2007), provides effective support for practitioners in helping to assess the progress children make between the ages of 0 and 60+ months. What practitioners need, however, are ways in which to gather these assessments:

● *Post-it note observations.* Record observations on Post-it notes as children are playing. Ensure you clearly record the child's name, the date, the time the observation started and finished, the context, and a judgement of what the child has achieved in reference to the 'Development matters' statements.

● *Analysing the visual.* Consider using digital images and video footage to make assessments of progress. These can be used in staff or team meetings to evaluate practitioners' judgements about what they are seeing. Before you undertake photography or filming of children, you must gain parents' and carers' permission.

● *Blah blah blah.* Listen to children as they play, making a note of key words, phrases and threads of conversations that show developments in knowledge, skills and understanding. Where possible or appropriate, record conversations with Dictaphones or tape recorders for analysis.

● *Parental informants.* Access the wealth of knowledge parents and carers have of their babies and young children by regularly talking *with* them about the progress their child is making in the setting and at home. Use this information to validate, extend or challenge progress records.

● *Process and product.* Make informed judgements using the EYFS on children's work such as models, drawings, paintings and mark making, in relation not only to the final product but also to the process they used in its production.

● *In summary . . .* Use the EYFS Profile to summarize achievements at the end of F2. Create your own profiles for children not in F2 in the form of portfolios as a visual and written record of achievements and progress.

Considering Celebrations of Achievement

Any achievements made in children's physical development should be acknowledged and the children given the appropriate recognition they deserve. If their success is noted, children will grow in confidence and self-belief, which is likely to motivate and encourage them to embrace new challenges and experiences. The question is: how can we celebrate this success?

- *The oldies are the goodies*. Children adore stickers – simple as that! Have some readily available so that you can physically acknowledge progress in individuals as and when it occurs.

- *Purposeful praise*. Work to ensure that your verbal praise is genuine, and specific to the child (that is, the child's name is mentioned), and that it comments on both ability and effort.

- *Wonder Wall*. Have a digital camera to hand so that you, or the children, can take images of individuals engaging in physical activities that show progress in their development. Print these and display them, labelling them with the child's name, the context, what they were doing and achieved, and the date. Before you undertake photography or filming of children, you must gain parents' and carers' permission.

- *Immediate certification*. Acknowledging achievements at the end of term may be useful for parents and carers during a parent consultation but it is worthless for young children as they are likely to have forgotten what they have achieved. Prepare child-designed certificates that can be given out for special achievements on the day the progress was actually made.

- *Peer praise*. Work to build an ethos that encourages children to praise their peers via smiles, pats on the back, thumbs up and hugs.

- *Proud parents*. Keep parents up to date with their child's achievements by speaking to them at the end of the day. Alternatively, text them or send notes home along with certificates via email or post.

Section 10: Developing Physical Development

The Great Outdoors

'There is a growing awareness that for the good of their heath, children need to be out and about more, with their friends, exploring the outdoor world in their own way' (Butler, 2008). This quotation beautifully encapsulates the content of this Idea: being healthy, being active and being outside.

- *Hide and seek*. Children love this game as it encourages running actions, stillness and movement into small spaces. Keep game play high by having more than one 'seeker' at a time. Other games to play include Tag, British Bulldog and Off-Ground Touch.

- *Fantastic footprints*. Encourage children to get their wellington boots muddy, creating different trails with their footprints. When the trails are dry, can the children run along them? Who can get to the end of their trail the quickest?

- *Rubbish mound*. Challenge children to help you build a mound of rubbish to beat the record set in the *Guinness Book of Records* by providing them with gloves, plastic bags and hand-operated 'pickers' so the children can safely go supervised around the woods, collecting packets, wrappers and cans.

- *Tunnel vision*. Get the children to run around with one child being 'It'. If 'It' catches one of the runners, that runner must stand still with their legs apart. The only way the runner can be set free is if another runner crawls between their legs.

- *Bulging boxes*. Give each child a small box in which they must put as many different things as they can find in the woods. Ensure that the children do not tear leaves off trees or rip plants and flowers out of the ground.

Working with Outside Agencies

Many practitioners are daunted at the prospect of having to provide quality Physical Development for the children they work with, particularly as they have to ensure quality in the other five areas of Learning and Development *at the same time*. It is important to remember that with the introduction of Every Child Matters, partnership work is advocated as the best way for providing the best for children, and this approach can be adopted when considering quality provision for Physical Development.

- *Other settings*. It is likely that there are other settings and infant or primary schools near to you. Consider making links with them, working in partnership to share practice, resources and experiences.

- *Local authorities*. Attend network meetings, speak with coordinators, consult with advisers and tap into programmes of continuing professional development.

- *Leisure centres*. Speak with staff members to ascertain facilities available, rates, and times suitable for your children to access equipment and space.

- *Secondary schools*. Young people in nearby secondary schools may be studying for their GCSE Physical Education qualifications. How might inviting them into your setting support not only them but also the development of your children? Pupils working for their Duke of Edinburgh Award would relish the opportunity to spend time with your children. Which aspects of Physical Development provision could they develop with or for you?

- *National sports bodies*. Make contact with the Association for Physical Education (AfPE; www.afpe.org.uk) or the Youth Sport Trust (www.youthsporttrust.org) and find out about the exciting projects taking place to raise the profile of physical activity for children and young people.

- *Local clubs*. Tap into the knowledge and skills of practitioners leading or working for gymnastics, cricket, football, tennis or running clubs, adapting practice to suit the needs of your children.

- *The NHS*. Consult with GPs, health visitors, school nurses, nutritionists and other medical personnel who have access to a wealth of knowledge and expertise in the field of healthy living and fitness.

- *Universities*. Trainee teachers need as much educational contact with children as possible to develop and hone their teaching skills. Might mentoring a student or inviting them in for some voluntary work be of benefit to them and you?

Tantalizing Topics

Many settings use topics as an effective way of 'chunking' learning and teaching into manageable blocks. The potential of topic work for Physical Development is vast and the suggestions below merely serve to illustrate some of the ways in which PD can become a reality under these headings.

- *Water*. Moving like bodies of water (lakes, fjords, streams, the sea, rivers and waterfalls) and forms of water (snowflakes, icicles, raindrops and hailstones) will help children to explore and experiment with a wealth of varied movements.

- *Weather*. Ask children to consider how they might move through snow, rain, sleet, heavy winds and blazing sunshine.

- *Space*. Moving like rockets, asteroids, stars, aliens, spaceships, planets and robots will support children in their imaginative movement play.

- *Timepieces*. How would *you* move like a watch? A cuckoo clock? A sand timer? A grandfather clock? A digital stopwatch? An alarm clock? Show children visual images of these timepieces and let their creativity flow.

- *Journeys*. Where will the children go – Australia? The centre of the earth? Outer space? Russia? How will they get there? Skip? Hop? Jump? What vehicles might they use to get there? Cars? Planes? Trains? The possibilities are huge.

- *Traditional tales*. Encourage children to explore the qualities of the movements of characters from different stories, for example the *tiptoeing* wolf, the *trip-trapping* Billy Goats Gruff, the *marching* dwarfs.

- *Jungle fever*. Animals such as monkeys, lions, tigers, gorillas and cheetahs, and the ways in which they move (swing, climb, sprint and bound), will provide endless hours of fun and activity.

A-starting and A-stopping

An important aspect of control in Physical Development is a child's ability to start and stop. This is often a neglected skill in early years settings, with little taught input being dedicated to it, so let's do something about this now.

- *React to the whistle.* Support children in being able to react to the number of times a whistle is blown – for example, 1 = start, 2 = stop.

- *Musical game play.* Musical statues and bumps are a great way to help children to understand the value of being able to start and stop in response to cues, especially in game-play situations.

- *Sound box.* Have a selection of musical instruments and a screen to hide behind. Shake a tambourine to stop the children and a pair of maracas to set them off again.

- *Time indications.* Use the day-to-day routine of the setting to teach children about starting and stopping. For example, tell them to listen for the bell when it is snack time or dinner time or home time.

- *Road safety.* Set up a pedestrian crossing in the outdoor play area with the bikes and trikes. Teach children when it is appropriate to start moving across the crossing and when they should stop.

- *STOP signs.* Continuing with the road safety theme, have some 'building work' role play going on, thus requiring a STOP/GO sign to be used to allow traffic to come and go under the direction of a workperson.

- *Green card/red card.* Have green and red 'referee' cards to hand as a way of stopping children in their play when they are engaging in inappropriate or dangerous behaviour.

Enriching Physical Development with ICT

Enriching PD provision means that practitioners need to introduce creative and innovative approaches, not only in their delivery but also in the children's experiences. They can do so successfully through the use of ICT.

- *Pedometer*. A pedometer is a wonderful device to see how active children are in the setting. Children will love wearing one, and they are available free with many breakfast cereals.

- *Digital camera*. Use a digital camera to show children different ways of moving, balancing and creating sequences of movements, such as run, walk and skip.

- *Stopwatch*. Provide children with easy-to-operate stopwatches so they can time each other in running races.

- *Metronome*. Although a metronome is primarily a piece of musical equipment, it is a useful device to help children to keep in time when performing actions in unison with others. It also helps to regulate the speed at which movements are made.

- *CD player*. A CD player is a splendid piece of equipment to create atmosphere and stimulate movement through sound. An iPod or MP3 player can act as a useful alternative.

- *TV, video and DVD*. Create a collection of videos and DVDs that encourage children to move, such as Barney or celebrity exercise videos.

- *Dance Mat*. Set up Dance Mat on a computer and expect a lot of fun as children try to dance in time with the music.

- *Software packages*. Although there are not many software packages specifically linked to PD for young children, there are screens and activities that can support learning about aspects of PD, such as dressing Teddy for exercise or selecting fruit for a healthy snack.

Physical Development During the Holidays

For many parents and carers, the thought of keeping their child 'occupied' over the summer holidays is quite daunting, yet the holidays are a perfect opportunity for the whole family to get involved in activities that encourage physical activity. Work to find ways of helping parents and carers to support their child's 'summer of movement'.

- *Fun at the park*. Local parks are now having National Lottery and local authority funding pumped into them so that children and adults have somewhere to kick a ball, throw a Frisbee, walk the dog and slide down the slide.

- *Walkies*. Take the dog for a walk, put the toy cat on a lead, fly the paper bird – do anything to get outside, move and get fresh air into the lungs.

- *Lovely leisure centres*. Visit the local sports centre to see what provision is made for young children. Crèches, mother and toddler groups, soft play hours and swimming sessions for the under-5s are just some of the activities on offer throughout the year.

- *Paddle in the sea*. The British tradition of a day out at the seaside should be kept alive as the potential for physical development is huge: swimming, walking, digging, running, and manipulating tools such as rakes.

- *Brilliant back garden*. Any garden space outside should be utilized for children to get out and play in. Bats, balls, paddling pools and slides are resources and features of a garden that will stay with a child for ever.

- *Strut that funky stuff*. A treasure trove of CDs are housed in more or less every household. Push the living-room furniture to the side, put on a track that makes you and your child want to dance and throw some shapes in the air with your hands.

- *Themed BBQs*. When the barbecues come out for the summer, invite friends and family around to an 'active' BBQ or a 'healthy' BBQ. Set out equipment that can be used by all to take part in a few sporty competitions.

Getting Parents and the Wider Family Involved in Physical Development

The EYFS Practice Guidance strongly advocates that parents should be seen as partners, and so practitioners and settings are striving to find successful ways to get them more involved in their child's development and learning. While support linked to aspects of CLL and PSRN is developed in most settings, few would evaluate their support for PD so positively. Until now, that is!

- *'Putting' parent helpers*. Utilize the skills of parent helpers by asking them to model and support children in their play such as swinging a plastic golf club or hitting a bat with a ball.

- *Weekend play*. Suggest to parents that they take their child to the local park or sports centre as a way of supporting the work engaged with in the setting during the week, for example designing new playgrounds, or water safety.

- *Talk about your physical play*. Parents are keen to know what their child has been doing at the setting, so encourage them to ask their child about what they have been doing *physically* through newsletters home, prompts around the room or verbal reminders.

- *Sports Day*. A number of settings are reluctant to organize sports days as they are deemed to encourage unhealthy competitive attitudes. Nevertheless, sports days are a great way for children to take part in physical activity along with the parents when it comes to the running races. Why not have a sports day where the children and parents have to collaborate throughout?

- *Leaflets galore*. Send out leaflets that advertise clubs, activities and opportunities for families to get involved in physical activity, for example local dance festivals, movement arcades and summer schools of physical activity.

IDEA

98

Raising the Profile of Physical Development

Practitioners are in a perfect position to raise the profile of PD because of their frequent access to adults and children. Finding ways to do this is the key to success. That is where this Idea fits in.

- *Table-top displays.* Designate a table specifically for parents and carers in the entrance where their children are dropped off and collected. Display 'physical' leaflets, flyers, pamphlets, brochures, magazines and web links so that parents and carers can take them or browse through them.

- *Everyone up.* Encourage parents and carers either to take part in group physical activity sessions or to visit the outdoor play area so that they can engage in purposeful play with their child, particularly at the start of a session during 'settling in' time.

- *Special guests.* Invite local sportspeople into the setting to talk to the children and parents about their skills, encouraging demonstrations and opportunities for children to get involved, either during or after the event. Examples include bowling balls (cricketers), kicking balls (footballers) and hitting balls with bats or rackets (tennis players).

- *Active Mark.* Visit www.teachernet.gov.uk and, wherever possible, work in collaboration with the children, their parents, carers and wider family members to achieve this mark of excellence for physical activity.

- *Physical activity portfolio.* Build a portfolio of pictures, drawings, images and writing about sessions, events and occasions when physical activity is driving learning, such as sports day, a sponsored run or get fit clubs.

- *Wonderful website.* If your setting is fortunate enough to have its own website, ensure that any physical activity that takes place is included on it. But remember: do obtain permission from parents and carers to photograph children.

IDEA

99

Being 'Innovatively Active' for Life

To promote and sustain quality Physical Development, practitioners in settings across the country are continually considering new and exciting ways to entice children into being physically active. The suggestions below are simply designed to be a bank of strategies that can be adopted in your setting with a little thought and planning.

- *Active . . .?* Clearly establish what your focus will be: Active play? Active sports? Active travel? Outdoor activities? General active living (for example, using stairs instead of lifts or escalators)?

- *Health visitor visits.* Use health visitors to talk to children and parents about safety in the sun, health and hygiene, and eating habits.

- *Healthy gardens.* Work with the children to build a healthy garden where they can grow organic vegetables and fruit, and regularly tend it with age-appropriate tools and equipment.

- *Coach visits.* Plan for local gymnastic coaches to visit your setting throughout the year, delivering pre-school gymnastic activities to build children's motor skills and develop their confidence.

- *TOP bags.* Visit www.youthsporttrust.org/page/top-programmes/index to see how the organized sharing of sports equipment bags between schools and settings through TOP Tots, TOP Start and TOP Play can promote a wonderful world of movement for children aged 18 months to 5+ years.

- *Fit zones.* Provide opportunities for family sessions to work together on yoga, 'push and pant' sessions, and outdoor adventurous activities, planned and delivered by the setting as part of its commitment to raising physical activity levels in the local area.

Physical Development and Life – it's time to *party!*

Children need to appreciate that Physical Development is a valuable and integral part of life, and there is no more perfect an opportunity to show this than when they play games at their friends' parties! You might like to play these games when you have the Christmas or end-of-year party at your setting.

- *Musical madness.* Play musical bumps, musical statues and musical chairs to develop reactions to music, allowing children to work at different levels and build their skills in stillness.

- *Balloon crush.* Spread inflated balloons all over the floor, setting children the task of bursting them all in the quickest time possible. If safety considerations concern you, then state that the children cannot *stand* on them. How are they going to burst them now?

- *Lots of lines.* Stand five children in a line with their legs apart. The child at the front of the line must crawl through the row of legs until they get to the end of the line. Once the first child has reached the end, the next child can set off. Have two or more lines at the same time so that there is a race on the go. Alternatives include having the child at the back coming down to the front, or a ball being passed up or down the line either through the legs or over the children's heads.

- *The oldies are the goodies.* Play Granny's footsteps, 'What's the time, Mr Wolf?' and Alphabet treasure hunts to develop movement, stillness and curiosity skills.

- *Races galore.* There are many kinds of races that children can take part in and enjoy: sack races, two-legged races, egg and spoon, and relay.

- *Safety islands.* A personal favourite. Provide each child with a pillow or a small carpet square, distributing these out on the floor. Have the children move around them until you shout out 'Shark's a-coming!' The children must dash to a free island, ensuring no part of their body has contact with the floor. Take one island away and play again.

A Random Selection of Simple Games

A bonus Idea! The best way I personally know to make children love physical activity is by having a bank of little games to play with children. These games act not only as purposeful activities but also as useful 5-minute fillers. Close your eyes, wave your finger over the page and randomly choose a good 'un.

- *Jack-in-the-box*. Ask the children to curl up into the smallest ball so they can fit into the imaginary box around them. On the count of three, let them pop out and bob about, laughing.

- *Body parts to the floor*. Ask the children to move around the indoor or outdoor space in different ways. For example, they could skip, hop, jump or sprint. All of a sudden, call out a body part, which the children need to put to the floor immediately, for example 'HAND!', 'EAR!', 'BOTTOM!'

- *Follow me*. Pair children up, labelling them A and B. (For younger children, ask one child to wear a ribbon on a tag.) Child A must move in different ways, and B must follow them, trying to copy their actions to the best of their ability. Then swap, so that A must now copy B's movements.

- *Spaceship play*. Develop intergalactic space role play by asking the children to use their body to represent different types of space vehicles when called out. For example, they could be rockets (arms pointing up together as they race around), alien spaceships (arms on hips, making BEEP-BEEP-BEEP noises) or battleships (arms bent out at right angles, making gun-blasting noises).

- *Running on the spot*. Get all the children to run around. Suddenly call out three children's names. These children must run on the spot while the rest of the group carry on running around them. 'Spots off!' releases the three children until another three names are called.

- *Puppetry play*. Move like a type of puppet – finger, hand, wooden, manikin, string, glove. Can they work out which one you are? Who is trying to be like Sooty? What about Muffin the Mule? Basil Brush? Rosie and Jim?

References

Butler, N. (2008) Freeplay network, available from: www.freeplaynetwork.org.uk (accessed 13 September 2008).

DfES (2003) *Excellence and Enjoyment: A Strategy for Primary Schools*. Nottingham: DfES Publications

DfES (2004) *Every Child Matters: Change for Children*. London: DfES.

DfES (2007) *The Early Years Foundation Stage*. Nottingham: DfES Publications.

Kit, Y. S. (2008) *Why Children Should Exercise*. Available from www. streetdirectory.com/travel_guide/39374/fitness/why_children_should_exercise. html (accessed 21 September 2008).

National Heart Lung and Blood Institute (2008) 'Star Sleeper, For Teachers: Why sleep is important'. Available from www.nhlbi.nih.gov/health/public/sleep/starslp/teachers/whysleep.htm (accessed 4 November 2008).

DATE DUE

GAYLORD

PRINTED IN U.S.A.